One very ordinary

One extra-ordinary God

A Memoire

By

Wendy S Sullivan

Written for and dedicated with much love to Jordan Mark, Ashleigh Ann and Keziah Jane. The future.

"What if we can only understand our purpose in life by allowing the stories of our lives to find their place in a bigger and more beautiful story, one we are called to not merely read about but participate in" **

** From "The God Story" by Alain Emerson & Adam Cox

CONTENTS

Foreword by Jason Swan Clark PhD

1. In the beginning
2. All change
3. Onwards
4. Deception
5. Betrayal
6. Can it get worse?
7. The beginning of Recovery
8. Extended Family
9. Endings and beginnings
10. Career Girl (1)
11. Career girl (2)
12. Moving On
13. Feeding in the field
14. Homelessness on the Horizon
15. The slippery slope
16. Singing a new song
17. Melodies, Harmonies and Rythmns
18. A home that no-one can take away
19. And so to now

NB All scripture quotations are taken from the New International Version of the Bible

NB Personal names, where used, have been substituted

FOREWORD

Most of us have people that no one else will ever know about. These people are not just part of the warp and weft of life but are key to vital moments and the seasons of life that made us who we are. Wendy Sullivan is one such person for me. I wish everyone could know about Wendy, and now they have the opportunity to do so with her memoir.

Wendy came into my life when I was twenty-eight, helping me find more of the Lord for the next twenty-eight years. She has been a prayer warrior, supporter, encourager, and friend for half my life. Everyone needs a Wendy in their life.

My own story has had its ups and downs and intensely painful moments, through which Wendy was ever present. Some of those moments I fear I would have been wholly overcome without her acceptance, love and care. Most of all, underneath everything Wendy brought into my life, more of Jesus was her priority for me. Wendy always helped me to encounter more of Jesus. And she did so having discovered Christ in her own life through some of the most awful circumstances. Wendy is a living epistle and testimony to God's furious, passionate, gracious love.

This memoir tells the story of an ordinary person, like you, and how God met them at every twist and turn of life. With every betrayal and trauma, Wendy reached for the Lord, and he sustained her. More than that, Wendy flourished and grew into someone who impacted the lives of many, including mine. In doing so, she became far from ordinary, just as God wants to affirm and grow you.

I commend her story to you. In its pages of God's faithfulness to Wendy, may you discover more of His for you. And may you find a little of Wendy Sullivan in your life too. Whoever you are, know that as you read her story, she would sit with you, listen to you, pray for you, and bring you to Jesus.

Jason Swan Clark, PhD

Director of the London Centre for Spiritual Direction

Chapter 1: In the Beginning

"In the beginning was the word...." Genesis 1:1

Beginnings are significant! The way I begin this book is important because it will probably determine whether or not you continue this journey with me!

My beginnings were unremarkable – as is so much of my life. But this book is not about what a remarkable person I am, nor is it about what a remarkable life I have led in the sense that, in the scheme of things, my life will alter the course of human history not one iota!

In fact as I begin my hope is that it will tell the story of a very ordinary life that nevertheless had the privilege of knowing the most remarkable God; the God of the Christian faith, the God whose plan and purpose for mankind is revealed through his son Jesus; Jesus of Nazareth; Jesus Christ, son of the living God, who lived, died and lived again in the nation of Israel 2000 years ago.

So, is this a bible study book then? No. Is it an argument for the truth of Christianity? Not really. It intends to be the story of how just one; one out of millions; one ordinary human life can experience the reality of that living God and his son Jesus.

So, the beginning……. I was born immediately post war – the second world war – in 1946, in the east Anglian town of Ipswich, to parents who were probably a bit surprised! They had been married for eighteen years; had a fourteen-year-old son and found themselves with a baby daughter! My parents had seen out the war years in Ipswich although both had been born in London, and because of my father's age, he had not been called up into the armed forces but had been an active member of the local Home Guard, so whilst I'm sure those war years were stressful, my immediate family was not grieving loss, as so many families were.

By the time I was three, my father's job in the Civil Service had taken him to St Albans in Hertfordshire and eventually my mother and I joined him and my brother there in a brand-new house which my dad had had built. This became the home I remember during my early school years, a comfortable, but unpretentious house, in a quiet Cul de Sac with a field at the bottom of our long garden and more fields at the top of the road. My brother had soon left home to do National Service in the Royal Air Force, and I look back at my childhood as being effectively one of an only child.

All in all, I had an uneventful childhood. 1950s Britain was in recovery mode and my childhood years were very aware of the effects of the war that had just ended, and the fears of the one that could begin as we entered the period of the "cold war". I remember the sense of threat in news bulletins and adult discussions around the tension between eastern bloc countries and western bloc countries which lasted until the fall of the Soviet Union in 1991.

I loved school and sailed through first Primary and then Junior School always comfortable at the top of the class in tests and exams and eventually passed my 11+ exam to go to the local Girls' Grammar School. That, however, was not to be as my father's job re-located him again, and my parents and I moved to Surrey (my brother was married by this time) where I started over, transferring my exam success to the local Girls' Grammar, in a totally new environment, with no existing friends, having left all my friendships behind in St Albans. Challenging times for an eleven-year-old!

Secondary school was in itself a lot more challenging and began to define me, sorting out my strengths and weaknesses, my preferences and dislikes, and my opinions! I realised I had limited affinity with maths and the sciences, whilst languages and literature floated my boat! I found I disliked sport and art but loved music and dance! I found I had a load of questions, about all sorts of things, and limited opportunity for suitable discussion opportunities. My family were not big into talking – well not about things that interested me – and my frustrations resulted in the typical sulky, withdrawn and somewhat stroppy teenager!

As life moved towards the beginning of the 1960s things were looking up; change was in the air, and it was an exciting time to be young! It was the birth of teenage culture, the hit parade, Bill Haley and Rock Around the Clock, then Elvis, and eventually the Beatles. I loved it all and was swept along with the tide of optimism. I had benefited from a good education and left school with good enough exam results to join the 5% of school leavers going on to university in the 60s, but I had no particular ambitions in that direction and opted to start earning some money instead. The beginning of 1965 saw me following in my father's footsteps and starting work as an Executive Officer with the Board of Trade at their spanking new office on London's Victoria street, right next to Westminster Abbey.

At the age of sixteen, I met a handsome young guy at a local church youth club, (not that either of us had anything to do with the church!) We were two essentially lonely young people, neither of whose home lives were particularly close or rewarding, who found a whole new world of love in each other and soon became inseparable. Eventually, we were both working in steady jobs and were keen to get on with life; to be together; to escape the parental home, and in those days that still meant getting married!

So, 1967 saw us tying the knot in the local parish church with bridesmaids, and hymns and prayers, and the organ playing the Mendelsohn bridal march. It was a beautiful April day, and it was everything I had dreamed my wedding would be. I had struggled with my conscience a little about getting married in church because in my teens I had very definitely come to the conclusion that there was no God. I had decided the Bible was myth, and that God was an outdated concept that early mankind had invented to provide answers for all the things they couldn't understand or explain! In 1960s Britian we no longer needed a God as we now had Science and Technology!

However, I did want to get married in a traditional old, stone, church building and I did want an organ, and I did want bells! So, I swallowed my vague niggles of conscience and walked down the aisle full of trust and optimism, and a new season began.

We started life together in a one-bedroom flat which was part of an old, converted mansion. We hadn't planned ahead beyond getting married and being together. We were both enjoying our jobs; and enjoying being young and in love and together; enjoying a sense of freedom with no real concern for the future; no real plans for houses, mortgages, or families. However, people say you never know what's round the corner, and we certainly didn't!!

Afterthought: At whatever stage of life we find ourselves, none of us can be sure of what is around the corner. Much as we like to kid ourselves, we are none of us fully in control of our destiny. We sometimes live in complete denial of what may be ahead; or maybe we live in a constant low-level anxiety about what might happen up ahead. We rarely live in complete peace about tomorrow.

2: All Change

"In their hearts humans plan their course, but the Lord establishes their steps" Proverbs 16:9

This book is not an autobiography: it is a memoire. It will not necessarily proceed on a consecutive timescale and is not comprehensive in detail but for now the year is 1969. I am married to my teenage sweetheart, and we are living in our first flat on the ground floor of a converted mansion house in Purley, Surrey.

Looking back, we were young to wed, but we had known each other 5 years before we did get married, having met at a local Methodist church youth club when we were both 16

We had soon realised that the other flats in our "mansion" were occupied by several other young couples, and we found ourselves getting to know one of those couple really well. Brent and Marcia were our age, but had been married longer, and had their first child already. We started getting together in the evenings over cups of coffee and doing a lot of talking! We discovered that Brent and Marcia had started going to a local Baptist Church, and that Marcia had grown up in a family that went to church, but had abandoned that practise when she had left home to work in London, Brent had not been to church before, but had started going with his wife because they wanted to have their little girl dedicated in church.

We found this all rather quaint. Neither of our families had gone to church, and as previously indicated, I in particular had quite a strong opinion that God did not exist; that in 1960's Swinging Britain, he was an outdated concept replaced by science and technology! I had steered clear of girls at school whom I knew were Christians and generally felt very discomforted around anything to do with church. We had got married in the local parish church, but only because I knew nothing about Registry Office weddings; had never been to one; and most definitely wanted the long white dress, an organ, hymns and church bells ringing!

Around the time that we were getting friendly with B and M, my sister-in-law introduced me to a series of novels by Dennis Wheatley which were about the occult and dark supernatural experiences. At the time, Dennis Wheatley was a hugely successful writer, selling a million copies of his books per year. I read avidly on the train to work every day and became fascinated by this dark world of adventure, and then an aunt who was a significant figure in my growing up years, began talking about visiting a Faith Healer seeking relief for her severe arthritis and this too began to fascinate me.

Eventually I gave in to my curiosity and arranged an appointment with the same Faith Healer as my aunt was seeing. He was kind and gentle and hooked me in with stories about my maternal grandfather who had died when I was 15 and who was apparently "looking after me" from the "Other Side". When I checked out his details about my grandfather with my mother, and found they were accurate, I was amazed!

So, in our coffee evenings with Brent and Marcia, I began to share about my experiences with the Faith Healer – and they began to talk to us about Jesus, and faith and belief and the Bible! Well, we argued! We disputed! I am ashamed to say we even ridiculed! I did NOT want to know about this! And truth to tell, was quite shocked that this lovely couple, who had come to be very important to us as friends, could actually believe this stuff!!

Around this time, to our mutual surprise, we found I was pregnant! As far as we were both concerned, I shouldn't have been – but I was! Not part of the plan at that moment in time and I was a bit scared! I was not sure that I was ready to be a mother – my husband took the news much more calmly! So, in my anxiety, I talked to the Faith Healer about it! And he assured me that my grandfather was looking out for me and that the pregnancy and delivery would be textbook! So natural and easy that I could have my baby at home!

Because we needed to move from our little mansion flat ahead of our baby's arrival, we had to sell the wonderful new car we had just bought in order to put a deposit on our first house, and no car meant I could no longer get to see the Faith Healer. My pregnancy proceeded normally but our son was a bit slow to arrive, so ultimately, I was admitted into hospital, there were complications, and our precious son was eventually delivered by emergency c-section to save his life. All very traumatic and not at all what Mr Faith Healer had led me to expect.

Those first few weeks of motherhood went by on automatic pilot. I had a perfect baby, who fed well, slept well and was strong and healthy, but his mum was mildly depressed, traumatised through the unexpected events surrounding the birth, and not quite sure who I was or what I was doing. Until, one morning, going in to pick my son up from his cot when he was about 5 weeks old, he turned his head, and his first ever real smile lit up his face on seeing me – and I woke up from my daze and fell in love!

From then on, I absolutely adored being a mum to this gorgeous child – and later to his equally gorgeous sister. I felt fulfilled in my marriage, my motherhood and my new little house - our first venture into home ownership. Although life had taken this unexpected turn, it was turning out surprisingly well.

Meanwhile, our friendship with Brent and Marcia continued, although we no longer lived so close, and one day, Brent announced to us that he had decided to "be baptised. "

"What do you mean, baptised, Brent? Isn't that for babies?" We were mystified!! Why would you want to do that? Over the next few weeks, on every possible opportunity, Brent would ask us if we would come to his baptism on a Sunday evening at the church and we would politely decline. However, I began to feel bad about his obvious disappointment. Were we being unreasonable? They were by now highly valued friends. Maybe we should go? No! The whole idea was vaguely embarrassing. And yet….. he kept asking.

Eventually, I hesitantly suggested to my husband that maybe we should go – and he still declined but suggested I should go, and he would stop at home with the baby.

So, on a dark and miserable November evening, I took myself off to this local Baptist Church with a sense of satisfaction that I was doing a favour for a friend! I remember justifying it with my husband by saying "Well at least it's not going to cost anything is it!" How little I knew!

I parked up and entered this church building which at first impression was warm and brightly lit and full of people! First surprise! I didn't think anybody went to church anymore! I squeezed into a pew beside Marcia and the proceedings began. We sang a couple of hymns which I vaguely remembered from school, then the guy who was apparently the Minister stood up in the wooden pulpit and began to talk about the Bible. I listened politely, determined to see this through for my friend. However, something strange was happening….

The guy in the pulpit was talking about Jesus. I knew a bit about Jesus from school. He was supposed to have been born to a virgin at Christmas; he was a sort of shepherd and went about healing people, but he died a horrible death, and he had always made me feel uncomfortable and as though I needed to avoid him.

But something weird was happening. The minister guy kept talking. I can't really remember anything about what he said. I think he was talking from the book written by John, but I can't remember specifically. What I can remember so very clearly is the feeling! It was almost a physical feeling. Have you ever been told some news that really shocked you so that you felt momentarily weak physically? Sitting in a pew in that church, next to my friend, on a misty November evening, I felt like that! Shocked! Really shocked! And gradually, as the voice in the pulpit continued to talk, I realised why I was feeling this sense of shock. I had been wrong!!!! Everything I thought about this man Jesus was wrong; completely wrong! It had never really occurred to me that this Jesus had been real; had really lived! I thought he was some sort of historic myth! But suddenly, what this man was saying I knew was true, and True with a capital T! I felt as though Truth itself had confronted me, convicted me of my error, and I was profoundly shocked. I physically felt the confidence that I had in my own version of truth was draining out of my head, my heart and my whole body. The arrogant platform I had built to stand on was destroyed under my feet, and my arrogant certainty lay in tatters around me.

However, powerful though this feeling was, it passed quite quickly, and I became aware of something sort of rising up in me from my feet upwards to my head! I couldn't have named it at the time, but I now know what was rising in me was certainty about this Truth; acceptance of this truth; confidence in this person Jesus; belief in the reality of what I was hearing; that Jesus was a real person in history, that he really had been crucified and died; that he really had risen from the grave and the really Big Truth I was hearing was that he did all of this – for me!

I felt physically weak and shaky, but so certain of what I now knew that I would have unhesitatingly followed my friend though the baptismal pool myself when we got to that part of the service! I felt that I wanted to physically let that water wash away all my years of arrogant disbelief so that I could start again, literally with a clean sheet! However, I was not given that opportunity; that came some months later.

I can't remember what interactions I had with either Brent or Marcia before leaving the church, but as I drove home that evening to my husband and baby son, I knew my life had changed irrevocably and would never be the same. I couldn't wait to go to church again the following Sunday!

From that day to this, and as I write that is coming up to 55 years, I have been a follower of Jesus. Truth is important to me. Despite storms and calamities; shocks and failures; mistakes and heartbreak, I have never regretted that decision to give in to a friend's persistent invitation.

Afterthought: Truth seems to have become so undervalued in current times. Public figures have been found to be lying quite blatantly and as a society we seem to accept that. Is that not a slippery slope? Does truth really not matter anymore?

Chapter 3: Onwards

"Practice these things, immerse yourself in them, so that all may see your progress" !Timothy 4:15

And so, I was now a Christian, a Believer, and six months later, at my own baptismal service, my husband had a similar experience to mine and he also then believed and received Jesus into his life and we became a Christian family and joined a church.

For my part, I was very aware of my ignorance, and I conceived a passionate desire to learn. The Bible had been a closed – and despised – book to me, but now, as our Minister, who was a very good Bible teacher, spoke week by week, I was both hooked and astonished as I began to fill in some of the gaps of my sketchy knowledge and dispense with some of my ignorant attitudes. I remember the wonder of the first Christmas that we spent in church and the deep joy and satisfaction of understanding the context of social Christmas traditions in the light of the truth in the biblical narrative.

Like most married couples, we were not beyond the odd disagreement! I remember one such occasion when we'd argued about something. We could both be pretty fiery, and definitely stubborn, and I certainly didn't like being wrong! We went to bed still arguing, and I was pretty miffed when my husband got into bed, turned out the light and was immediately asleep, whilst I was expecting resolution to the argument! I remember that I got up and went back downstairs and picked up my Bible and it fell open and some verses jumped off the page at me. I had been a Christian about two years at this point and apart from that first unreal night at Brent's baptism, my experience had been cerebral, about learning, about absorbing knowledge, but that evening it felt different. I couldn't have explained why; I now know it was a "God moment", a personal touch of the Holy Spirit. The verses that jumped out at me, I didn't understand. They were in a book of the Bible I'd never noticed before – it is a very small one! - but I knew they were about my husband, my marriage, and I knew they were important.

The verses said this:

15 *Perhaps the reason he was separated from you for a little while was that you might have him back forever— 16 no longer as a slave, but better than a slave, as a dear brother. He is very dear to me but even dearer to you, both as a fellow man and as a brother in the Lord.* (From Paul's Letter to Philemon)

Remember those verses! They will feature again further on!

We had a second child, our beautiful daughter, and settled into a steady family life which we both found fulfilling. We were babies ourselves still in our spiritual experience, but eager to learn and enjoying the journey. I began to read Christian books. I remember reading "The Cross and the Switchblade" by David Wilkerson which had just been published, followed by "Run Baby Run" by Nicky Cruz, both of which made a strong impression on me. This God of the miraculous was still fairly distant to me though, and apart from my supernatural experience at that baptismal service, the only other such encounter I had during this period was an unbelievable one in many ways, that only I experienced.

I was doing some handwashing at the kitchen sink – a couple of delicate items that I would not entrust to the washing machine of that generation! One of these was a very precious silver-grey fine gauge mohair cardigan that was painstakingly knitted for me by my mum. Another item was a black t-shirt that I was hand washing because I knew the dye was probably dodgy. I knew that. So, I was taking great care to keep the silver- grey and the black separate from each other. At least I was….. until I wasn't. Somehow, they had nudged up against each other and there on the beautiful delicate silver grey was a large black stain. Oh no! I ran the tap and frantically started dunking the silver-grey cardigan in and out of the water, soaking it, gently squeezing it, soaking it again, all to no avail, the stain did not budge. I was reading "Run Baby Run" at the time and had in mind the amazing things that God apparently did – so I found myself praying! Not very coherently, just "Oh God, please, Oh God help, Oh God, Oh God!"

And then after at least five minutes of fruitless dunking and rinsing with absolutely no affect, there was no black stain! None whatsoever! Not a lessened black stain that would encourage me to keep dunking – but absolutely no trace of a stain! I was stunned! One minute it was there, and the next it was not!!

And after it had really sunk in, I was humbled. A little miracle! Why God? Why would you do that? Just for me? Such a small unimportant thing in the face of world need!

And yet, that small unimportant thing that God in His grace did for me that day, was laid down in my experience as foundational to my trust in God's understanding and care for me as an individual, and for all of us who remain individuals in His sight.

A couple of years in, we became very friendly with a couple in our church who talked about a dream of buying a large property in the area to use for Christian fellowship, maybe even a small Christian community. Eventually their dream was realised and they became the owners of a very large house locally called Holly Hill complete with several acres of land. Just after their fourth child was born, they moved in and faced an uphill challenge to manage the 15 bedrooms and four lounges not to mention the huge kitchen, orchard, rose gardens and paddock! Our two children were now both in school, I wasn't working and my husband worked shifts, and was often around in the daytime, so we offered our services in practical support. The property had been empty for quite a long while and had latterly been in use as a nursing home, so it was indeed an uphill task to restore it to something like a family home, and we threw ourselves into helping where we could.

As the months went by, our own home and garden began to suffer as all our spare time was spent at Holly Hill. It became apparent to all of us that maybe, only maybe, we should be selling up and moving in making the dream of a Christian Community a reality. It was a big decision. New and inexperienced in it though we were, we turned to prayer to try and discern whether or not this was God's purpose or just human beings putting two and two together and making five! Disappointingly, there were no thunderbolts of lightening or voices from heaven but gradually over a period of months, we talked and prayed with other members of our church, talked to our children (who loved the idea) and decided to put our house on the market to see what would happen. One verse of scripture that did seem to speak to me at that time, I remember very well. It is from Matthew's gospel:

"And everyone who has left houses or brothers or sisters or father or mother or children or fields for my sake will receive a hundred times as much and will inherit eternal life." Matt 19:29

That seemed reassuring at the time and our house sold very quickly. We packed up and moved a couple of miles up the road and into Holly Hill as residents.

Life in community was busy! It was challenging and very rewarding! We were at minimum a household of ten, but frequently we were more than that. We always ate breakfast as individual families, but shared lunch and dinner together around the large kitchen table. The other mum was a cordon bleu trained chef – which was a bit intimidating! We agreed a routine where one week she did all the cooking, and I managed all the laundry; and the next I would cook, and she would wash! That rationalised the use of the kitchen and laundry room and once I had acclimatised to cooking for a minimum of ten all the time, it worked very well!

The six children of the joint household, three boys and three girls, had a wonderful time!! There was always someone to play with and masses of space to occupy. They even discovered a secret passageway that went under the house from the cellar! It was the late 70's and long skirts were in. We discovered an old croquet set in the house and then held wonderful afternoons of croquet with the ladies elegantly wielding their mallets as their long skirts swept over the grass! Very Howards End!! I also fondly remember weekend afternoons in summer sitting in a circle on one of the lawns, adults, children and various visiting young people from local churches, with a two-foot-high mound of home-grown broad beans in the middle as we shucked them, and someone played choruses on a guitar and we all sang! Very 70s!!

We adults met together most mornings to start the day in prayer together and at times we were joined by the people the Lord seemed to send our way at different times to stay short or long term. We were still attending a local church and often hosted larger events. It was a time of subtle unrest stirring in the wider church. The 2023 film "Jesus Revolution" gives the background story which originated in America where a spiritual awakening amongst the younger generation was underway giving rise to the Jesus People movement and the turning of many young people to Jesus.

Churches in Britain were being stirred with an unrest that was looking for more of the reality of a supernatural God. The person of the third member of the Trinity, Holy Spirit, was becoming much talked and written about and Christians were expressing a hunger for more – although I don't think many actually knew what they meant by that!

We at Holly Hill began to question the predictable rhythm of our own church life and we also began to host some interesting people from the forefront of what God was doing – if indeed He was doing it! We had a young woman stay with us for a weekend who was on a first trip home from Hong Kong where the Lord had called her to work with the gangs and drug dealers of the Walled City there. The book she published shortly after made her famous, and her resulting long-term ministry in Hong Kong is now legend. We also hosted a young man, his family, and about 30 members of a brand-new congregation that had come out of local churches in the Crawley area seeking this "more". The young man and our guests went on to found one of the biggest new church movements that spread rapidly, planting churches across the nation up until this present day.

There was definitely something stirring and whilst I didn't understand it, I gradually became aware of a stirring going on in my own heart. It was by now almost ten years since I had

had my life changing encounter with Truth in the person of Jesus Christ. My life had certainly been impacted. I had learned a lot; I was hugely impacted by the truth and relevance of the Bible; I was bowled over by the example across the Gospels of the love and mercy and truth presented by Jesus; I had sought to respond to God in leaving our home, uprooting our family, in what we felt was obedience to this revelation….. and yet, something was missing.

Over a period of months, I gradually began to identify that what I was sensing was a growing dissatisfaction with myself! I began to identify that what I was feeling was a sense of concern about my own lack of change! Ten years of being a Christian, so, shouldn't I be changing? Shouldn't I be growing more like Jesus as the Bible says I should? And yet, in truth, I knew I was just as selfish, just as opinionated, just as short sighted as I had always been! That wasn't right!!

I began to wonder about this "experience of the Holy Spirit" that people were talking about. I had some talks with my Minister about it but came away un-helped. I too was restless. And it turned out, I was vulnerable too.

Afterthought: "Church" means different things to different people. To some it's about buildings and as a nation we have a wonderful heritage of parish churches amazingly constructed in days gone by in each village and town, as well as magnificent cathedrals built to glorify and honour God in ways which astound us given that they were built way before industrial equipment and highly trained architects. To others, church is rule and regulation, ritual and rites. Tragically to yet others it represents abuse, hypocrisy and manipulation. But if we can set those judgements aside, we can find churches that are truly seeking to build on the original blueprint.

Chapter 4: Deception

"Here on earth you will have many trials and sorrows. But take heart...."John 16:33 NLT

About this time, my sister-in-law, and closest friend, (she and her husband had come to the Lord at my husband's baptismal service continuing a sort of family chain reaction!) started talking about a minister she had heard of, who ran a Full Gospel Ministry and who gave appointments to people one to one to help them in their walk with God. She had met people who knew him and were benefitting. This information dropped into the middle of my restlessness, self-dissatisfaction and doubts and stayed there. Hmm. Perhaps this would be helpful. My own minister couldn't seem to understand my need. I talked the matter over with my husband and together we agreed there was no harm in me making an appointment to meet this minister.

I eventually drove into South London and met The Leader. It transpired he lived in a biggish house with a small community set up which resonated with our own living circumstances at

Holly Hill. He was an imposing figure; tall and well built; and he was blind. He was therefore quite dependant on some of the young people, including his own sons and daughter, who lived in the house. His wife was crippled with severe arthritis and very confined in her mobility. He put me at ease and asked me some questions, getting me talking, and then really listened to me as I sought to explain my review of my Christian experience so far and my sense of frustration with myself. It was helpful to be taken seriously and listened to.

Thus began a pattern of going over to South London quite regularly to see The Leader and coincidentally to get to know some of the other members of the extended household and also members of his wider fellowship, which it turned out was centred in several locations around London and which met together weekly on Saturday evenings in Kent.

I was quite open about my involvement with this leader and by then my husband had also met him and spent time with him. Imagine our surprise therefore when it was made clear to him by the husband of the couple with whom we shared community, that he needed to stop me going on my trips to South London! There followed some difficult discussions. My husband was very resistant to being told what he should and shouldn't allow his wife to do, particularly without good reason, and no good reasons were offered! This was tricky! At the end of the day, for all our success in living together in community for two years, we did not own the house. The other family did, and we were effectively lodgers. The situation rapidly, and very sadly, became untenable. We needed to move on – but where to? We had given up our place on the property ladder to move into Holly Hill, and the middle 70s witnessed a property boom as the mortgage market took off and house prices exploded. The 3 bedroomed semi-detached house we had sold for £11,000 in 1977 was now just over two years later worth nearer £20,000, which left us struggling for sufficient deposit to buy again. It was a serious crisis for us, and we prayed hard. It's a given fact that most of us pray with the most intent when we are in trouble or need or both!

I remember at that time two quite unrelated people came to me offering a "word from the Lord" in the shape of the same scripture from the Book of Revelation and the letter to the church in Philadelphia.

"These are the words of him who is holy and true, who holds the key of David. What he opens no one can shut, and what he shuts no one can open. 8 I know your deeds. See, I have placed before you an open door that no one can shut. I know that you have little strength, yet you have kept my word and have not denied my name." Revelation 3: 7-88

I remembered the scripture from Matthew that I had had on my mind when we were deciding whether to move and the promise it seemed to give for those who gave things up for the gospel, and then this new scripture seemed to me to confirm that the door the Lord had opened for us, no-one would shut; that the promise from the Matthew scripture would still hold good. That was comforting.

Nevertheless, we were struggling. The need to move was pressing and our options very limited. We had to consider the usual things – the children's schools, the proximity of our parents, the locations of my husband's job and, hardest of all, the financial sacrifice we had made that we could not redeem.

During this time, we both, individually, had meetings with The Leader and, to our surprise, he came up with a potential solution to our dilemma. He explained that his fellowship ran a charity that had financed and now owned several houses, each in the location of one of the scattered fellowship groups. He went on to say that there were a group of people in our area, ourselves included, who were looking to an alternative to their current church and needed a central meeting point. So, the suggestion was that this charity would finance the purchase of a house in our locality which would become that community hub for a new fellowship group under his leadership. Our current experience of living in community would be ideal experience for that setup.

We understood that the house would be a gift; that we would be responsible for all running costs and upkeep; and could stay there as long as we were serving the purposes of the fellowship. It seemed like an amazing answer to prayer, and a validation of the scriptures I had been hanging on to. We were then tasked to find a reasonably spacious four bedroomed house in a suitable location. This seemed an unbelievably amazing opportunity. But I was beginning to believe that this God of Truth that I had met was so true to His word that He would do amazing things! Even for us!!

Things moved amazingly quickly and within 6 weeks we were ready to move from Holly Hill to our new home.

Two days before moving day, my husband took a call from The Leader that pulled the rug from under my feet. There had been a change of plan, in that the trustees of charitable trust that was buying the house had found a legal problem and they could not buy the house in our name. it would be bought in the name of the trust, and we would still be able to live there as promised as long as we were adhering to the goals and principles of the trust.

To say that I was uneasy is a massive understatement! I was turned upside down and inside out. It didn't feel right! It wasn't what was agreed! And yet, we were due to move, the children had places in a new school, we were under pressure to get on with this move! For the very first time in my life, I did the classic not being able to sleep. I tossed and turned, then paced the bedroom. I talked to God. I was cross. I was disappointed. I was deeply, deeply disturbed that this was not right. That we were making a mistake. I was frightened.

My husband, on the other hand, was peaceful! He was a bit disappointed, yes, but not unduly concerned. He urged me not to worry, that he was there for me, I needed to trust him, and more importantly, that God was with us and would take care of us. This was unusual. It was usually me that was the one who was stronger in faith and more open about my understanding of God, but I had been praying for him to lead in our faith commitment, and that prayer at least seemed to be being answered, so I decided to trust my husband's judgement, step away from my fears and follow my husband's lead.

We moved; settled the children into a new school and began to settle into being a nuclear family again. We called our new home "Philadelphia" based on the scripture we'd been given and in trust of the "open door that no-one could shut". We were bruised from what had happened to end our Holly Hill experience, but closing in ranks as a family was comforting – and we were soon to meet a new community of friends who would become our extended family.

A new chapter had begun, and we were now hosting a group of five families complete with eleven children and four young singles as we came out of previous church experiences and began to be part of The Leader's scattered Gospel Fellowship.

It was intense. Everybody met at our house on Sunday mornings, and Wednesday evenings. Everybody went to a whole fellowship gathering in Kent on a Saturday evening. All the women met on a Thursday morning; and all the children met – at our house- on a Wednesday afternoons. In the middle of all that, each of us had individual appointments with KL on a regular, usually weekly basis. One of the other women was designated Leader of our group, but everything actually happened at our house.

Our meetings were unstructured except that we all had a copy of the same hymn book and half an hour or so before each meeting, we would get a phone call from one of the people who lived with The Leader giving the reference for the scripture passage to be studied on that occasion.

Looking back, the positives were mainly threefold:

- The intensity of regular gatherings with the same people fostered some really close, supportive and valued relationships
- Because there was never any led teaching in our meetings (apart from the joint Saturday evening ones), we unwittingly became dependent on Holy Spirit to lead us. I don't think any of us would have been able to admit to that at the time, but the fact was, we were often confronted with a random scripture passage which none of us knew. We had no tools and very little experience, but as we sat in our circle, one by one thoughts would be tentatively shared, expanded, and gradually light would begin to dawn over the words we were reading, and we found the truth that was written there. God revealed Himself to us through his word as He always does when the reader is a seeker as well. I for sure grew in my knowledge of the bible at that time in an amazing way because an amazing God has gifted us with the presence of His Spirit through the sacrifice of His son.
- Our children had strong and stable community around them. Other adults that knew them and would protect them, and across the wider fellowship, numerous friends who were also living this type of faith

commitment with their families. They also had friendship and investment from the young singles who were frequently in our home playing snooker, darts or table tennis. (equipment all provided by the fellowship).

However, there were clouds over the horizon too. I'm basically a "people person", mildly extravert, both an inward and outward processor, the close relationship and involvement with the wider group of people was satisfying. Being at the centre of everything, whilst not really leading, was confidence building. But deep within, I knew there was something uncomfortable that had been sitting somewhere in my subconscious since the phone call that changed the status quo over the ownership of the house. It was very small, and I couldn't define it or name it, but it was lurking and it fed a dim sense of unease. Outwardly, I knew our wider families didn't like it - particularly when we all had to leave family celebrations on Christmas Day in the afternoon to go to a main meeting in Kent. I knew our old friends Brent & Marcia were uneasy although nothing was really said. And I knew that our former community at Holly Hill had had their reasons for asking us to leave. If only they had voiced them clearly!

But we had a home, the children were happy and settled, it could be worse!

And then it was.

Afterthought: We live in a culture that bombards us with a thousand different voices. Everyman and his dog have an opinion, and the internet and social media allow them to voice it and the cacophony resulting can be overwhelming. Alongside that none of us, no not one, is infallible. The things we listen to influence us, affect our decisions and change us, for better or worse. So, once again, truth becomes important. Not anyone and everyone's version of truth, but Truth itself.

Chapter 5: Betrayal

"The heart of a man plans his way, but the Lord establishes his steps "Proverbs 16:9

We were content. The children were doing well. Our son was a talented sportsman; a child who did well at most things he tried and was a huge blessing. His dad was so proud of him and supported him all the way through junior league football. Our daughter loved her dancing lessons and all things girly and was a joy to both of us. We loved being parents. We had occasional spats as most families do, and a serious breach of trust in our relationship three years before that we had worked through, and I felt confident and secure in our family unit which was completed by our handsome and much adored red setter dog! We did things together as a family; lots of country walking adventures with the dog and family holidays in the Borrowdale Valley in Cumbria which to this day sits in all our memories as a happy place!!

My husband was a serving police officer. In April 1981 trouble broke out in Brixton London which went down in history as the Brixton Riots. Young men from the Afro-Caribbean community were taking out their frustrations resulting from the racial discrimination and in the increased use of stop and search in the area. Anger boiled over and the local police were the target. It was grim. On Saturday 11th April, since dubbed as "Bloody Saturday", the following were recorded: 279 injuries to police officers, 45 injuries to members of the public, over a hundred vehicles burned including 56 police vehicles, 150 buildings were damaged and thirty of those were burnt out.

All police leave was cancelled, and my husband was in the thick of it. We hardly saw him at home for three or four days. At one stage he later told me that he was in Railton Road outside The George pub, which had been set on fire. He said he had a colleague either side of him and the mob in front of them were forcing them backwards into the burning pub. One of his colleagues took a brick in the face and fell, the other also was hit and my husband found himself alone between the mob and the fire and he had no recollection of what happened next or how he got out.

He was exhausted and stressed, was not sleeping well, having nightmares and was generally not himself. I was not unduly worried as I thought he could take a few days off when things had quietened down and rest, and he'd be ok.

Ten days or so later, he was late home from a late shift in the evening – pre mobile phones this – and I was in bed but not asleep when he came in. I asked him what he'd been up to to be so late and to my surprise he said he'd driven up to a local viewpoint "to think". Not like him. He then proceeded to tell me that he'd taken the decision to leave. Leave? What, leave the job I asked? No, he replied. A decision to leave you!

There followed the most traumatic and distressing five weeks that I had ever experienced up to that point in my life.

My husband became a stranger overnight. He moved into the spare bedroom; he was cold and distant; he began receiving phone calls from people I didn't know or who wouldn't identify themselves; our building society books disappeared. He was uncommunicative, cold and distant. I was confused, angry and then desperate.

I begged, I pleaded, I raged, I cried. I demanded to know if he was having an affair. No, he wasn't, was the adamant reply.

He became aggressive and defensive, breaking my little finger as he wrested the phone from me on one occasion when I was demanding to know who was on the other end of the call. There was also an occasion when I demanded to know if the issue was about God and the fellowship, because, I said, and I truly meant it at the time, if that's the issue, I can give up God, I can live without God, but I can't live without you!

I have never forgotten his response. He told me that he would never let me do that. That God was right for me – but not for him.

I've since been really ashamed of that particular tactic – but I meant it and would have renounced God, and everything associated if it had meant my husband stayed. I adored him and whilst my belief in God and his gift to me of salvation through his wonderful son Jesus was by then a huge part of my life; it was an added extra in comparison with my marriage. That was a necessity to me.

I was desperate. Hurt and frightened and helpless. I turned to my friends, and of course to The Leader. However, about the time my husband had made his devastating announced, we in the fellowship had been told that The Leader was going on an indeterminate fast to pray for individuals and situations going on in the fellowship at that time. I managed one phone call with him straight away, during which he was strangely unhelpful, and then he became unavailable as he had taken to his bed with the weakness of fasting.

I was living in some sort of nightmare. Internally, I was panic struck, angry, frightened, insecure; and outwardly I was managing life as usual as far as the children were concerned; taking them to school, picking them up from school, preparing meals, taking them to football, ballet, etc. The ordinary routine of our family life. I said nothing to my parents, or wider family. Only those closest to me in our fellowship knew. I think I thought the situation would play itself out. come to nothing; blow over.

It was the day of the local schools swimming gala at a local pool. Our son was swimming for his school and although my husband was due to be on duty, he would always manage to "be passing by" if one of the children were involved in something important. But the swimming progressed, our son swam a winning race, and there was no sign of his dad. We got home about nine o'clock that evening, and as I opened the front door, I stopped short. Something was wrong. I looked at the coat rack in the hall, and my husband's coats were missing. I flew upstairs to our bedroom, and yes, all his stuff had gone.

I found a note on the kitchen table telling me that he had moved out to a bedsit, he wasn't going to give me an address, that he was going to Greece on holiday the next day with friends from work; that I could use the car whilst he was away but he would take it on his return; that when the bills arrived, I could phone him (at work) and if he had the money, he'd give me some and if he hadn't he couldn't. And that was it. It was the 3rd of June 1981.

I got the children to bed somehow and then phoned a friend who immediately came over and in fact stayed the whole night with me because she was so concerned for my state.

The next morning, I had to tell my two precious children that Daddy had gone away, and that I didn't know when he'd be coming back. I'm sure I didn't do that completely right; I don't know how you do break news like that in the best way. I do know, they never saw me at my worst, and I do know that I never vented my various phases of anger, grief, anxiety on them.

That first morning, I walked them to school as usual with the dog. It was a beautiful morning, and as I walked home, I attempted to communicate with God in prayer but when I got indoors the heaviness of despair was so great, I went back to bed. I lay in our bed sobbing and overcome with fear for the future. I couldn't cope on my own. From the age of sixteen, I had been part of an inseparable couple. I had never had to be me as a grown up. I had always been us. I was without hope.

I remember very clearly lying in bed huddled under a duvet although it was a lovely June morning, shivering, sobbing, and gradually becoming aware of a sense of wanting to die. It was the easy way out. I couldn't face the future, so the easy thing to do would be to do away with that future. I saw myself hanging over the edge of a precipice and below was a deep, deep, dark abyss. I was hanging over it headfirst and everything in me wanted to hit the bottom and oblivion. No more pain, no more fear, no more worry. I wanted to fall into that darkness. But… someone was hanging on to my ankles….. someone was stopping me from falling…..and I instinctively knew it was Jesus. I found myself saying out loud over and over "please let me go…. please let me go…. please let me go". But I also knew He wouldn't.

Gradually, I calmed down and began to think more clearly. Gradually through that morning in bed, my storm-tossed perspective began to find a better level and I knew, knew with absolute certainty, that I could not be selfish enough to take the easy way out and leave my children with no mother as well as a father who had deserted them. That I had no idea how I was going to cope, but that I was a mother and there was no escaping that. I would not let my children down. They needed me.

Two days later, to the complete shock and bewilderment of all the people in our house fellowship, and beyond, The Leader of our fellowship had died. He had apparently been fasting for three weeks or so. Another enormous shock, not just for me but for all the people I loved and was close to in our little house fellowship, and beyond to the people we had got to know in the fellowship further afield. There was little explanation for his death, and it had an air of mystery about it. And so, I found myself without a husband and without the Minister on whom I depended for counsel and advice.

Life staggered on, as it does. I found it hard to believe how much physical pain I was in without having any medical condition. I couldn't eat, I couldn't sleep, I lost about two stone in weight in about three weeks. My heart was broken, and it hurt; physically hurt.

My husband came back from Greece and took the car. The children were quiet and subdued. I don't believe my son in particular, ever really processed it. He was 11 years old and emotionally quite mature; mature enough to recognise that I was struggling, even though I did my best to keep it under wraps. Close friends commented to me that he was being very protective of me, even though I was trying to protect him from my real pain. I think with today's greater understanding of human wellbeing; I should probably have been more real with the children and thus encouraged them to be more aware of their own needs at that time.

A bit later on in that summer, the children were going away for a week to a summer camp arranged by the wider fellowship. I was absolutely dreading that. The children were my raison d'etre and the thought of a week on my own without them terrified me. I had never been on my own. I got married straight from my parent's home. I had never been solitary.

The week came and off they all went in great excitement. The weather was lovely, warm and sunny. The day before, I had been walking the dog and pondering the week ahead, when I found some words running through my head like a record that was stuck. "Arise my love, my fair one, come away". Strange. It then occurred to me that maybe they were from the Bible. When I got home, I found the old Bible Concordance I had bought from a second hand book shop (it was a long time before Google!) and found the words. They come from a book in the bible called Song of Solomon and the words that were relevant are these:

My beloved speaks and says to me:
"Arise, my love, my beautiful one,
  and come away,
for behold, the winter is past;
  the rain is over and gone. Song of Solomon 2: 10-11

The words played over and over in my mind. I didn't remember specifically ever reading them but gradually I became confident in the thought that the words came to my mind from God, and I sort of knew that it was Jesus speaking to me.

The week unfolded. I had decided I would do some decorating whilst the children were away to give me some focus, and as I got on with that, windows open to the lovely weather outside, just the dog for company, I began to sense this voice that had said "Arise my love my fair one" become a quiet presence accompanying me in my solitude. To my total surprise, I felt moments of peace during that week. I didn't feel so desolate and alone as I had expected. I even glimpsed momentarily a sense of wellbeing.

I painted walls, had coffees with other fellowship friends, walked the dog …. And all of a sudden, the week I had so dreaded was over and I was collecting the kids and bringing them home.

Life resumed and the reality of being a single mum with a painfully wounded heart kicked in again. It was time to go back to school and it was a milestone for my son as he was transitioning to secondary school. I now had no car, so he had to negotiate travelling on the bus and I began to juggle being single handed with children in different schools on different timetables and all the adjustment that takes. And meanwhile, there was no contact from my husband.

And, meanwhile, I had no income. I had my £13 per week Family Allowance and that was all. The fact that I was not having to pay any rent excluded me from claiming State Benefit, but I was liable for gas and electricity bills for a four-bedroom house plus food and other living costs. The average income at the time was £710 per month, so I was well below average. Could I have gone out and got a job? Well, I could have tried, but I was such a wreck, I doubt that I would have coped. I had completely lost confidence in myself, I felt a total failure in life. And above all, I was prioritising the children, and Mum suddenly going out to work for the first time in their lives was not what they needed.

Just a couple of weeks into term, it was my son's 12th birthday. I had made arrangements to borrow a friend's car for the evening, I had scraped together some money and was due to take him and three friends out in the evening to a Happy Eater diner which was some miles away, but the "in place" to go at the time!

The morning of his birthday, after the children were in school, my husband rang from a call box to say he wanted to see our son after school. This was the first call I had had and the first attempt for him to see the children. I explained that he couldn't as I already had arrangements in place but that he could see him the following day after school. He started insisting that he wanted to see his son and became quite unpleasant. I stuck to my guns and the conversation ended with him saying that if I wouldn't cooperate, he would pick the boy up from school and I may not see him again,,,, and putting the phone down!!!

I was left shocked and feeling threatened. I pondered what to do. I could ring the school and ask them to safeguard my son – but I knew that so soon into a new school, he would be devastated at being singled out for anything – particularly in these circumstances. Eventually, I arranged to borrow my friend's car earlier than planned and was myself right outside the school gate well before they were due to come out. He came out pretty promptly and was surprised to see me there but started to get into the car. As he did, my husband screeched up behind us as I accelerated away. There followed the most unbelievable drive as he tailgated us away from the school, actually bumping us once or twice. I was terrified but trying to maintain a calm exterior and think what to do. I was frightened to go home. This was not a man I knew, and I therefore couldn't predict what he would do. My sister-in-law and her family lived very close to us, and I would drive past her house to get to ours. There was every chance her husband would be home, and she had been collecting my daughter from school along with her own children. I prayed that her husband's car would be on the drive and explained to my son that as soon as we got to auntie's house, he should jump out and ring the doorbell. He did that just as the other car was screeching up behind us and we were both inside the house as my husband was getting out of his car.

My sister-in-law's husband had answered the door and ushered us in and then confronted his brother-in law who was clearly very worked up. He demanded to see his son, and was calmly told "No, not until you have calmed down". At that my husband took the birthday card he was holding and ripped it to shreds, including the ten-pound notes that were inside it. He left the pieces on the doorstep and stormed off.

We held it together and went off for our Happy Eater experience with my daughter and the four lads. When we got home about 9 o'clock, my brother-in-law had suggested that he should come round for a bit in case there was any further trouble. We had not long been in, and the children were just upstairs getting ready for bed, when the doorbell rang, It was my husband, once again demanding to see his son.

There followed a very unpleasant scene which is etched on all our memories. Because he was refused entry whilst he was angry, he proceeded to walk round the house banging on all the windows. The dog went mad and was barking furiously whilst both the children were in my son's bed frightened and upset because this was not the father they knew and loved. Eventually, we had no option but to call the police – my husband was warned that we would do so if he didn't leave. That of course had serious consequences for him as a serving police officer and the other consequence was that both the children were adamant that they did not want to see their dad because they were frightened.

How had we got here? How in a few short months had our stable family life come to this?

Afterthought: I truly believe that the worst pain human beings suffer is not the pain of torture or cancer, but that of rejection. Two of my closest friends over the years were both widows when we met. The pain of their bereavement and grief was huge for both of them. But they agreed that at least they did not have to live with the fact that their husbands had chosen to reject them and their marriage vows. Jesus, endured false accusation, scourging, mocking and the unbelievable pain of crucifixion in silence. The only time he gave voice to pain was when he felt that His Father had turned his back on him in rejection.

Chapter 6: Can it get worse?

"Hear my cry, O God, listen to my prayer" Psalm 61:4

Recovering from the birthday disaster took a while. The children appeared to bounce back and life resumed its new pattern without a father in the house. The fellowship was also trying to bounce back from the sudden and dramatic loss of its leader. The fellowship leader's adult sons had stepped into the leadership role and the routines carried on…. For a while. One of the senior men in the fellowship was also one of the trustees of the associated charity which owned the house we were living in. Over the last couple of years that we had been part of the fellowship, I had become particularly close to his wife and my son was particularly friendly with her three sons. They lived down in Kent, but we were frequent visitors to each other's homes.

After my husband left, they were particularly supportive, and the wife and I often met for lunch and a chat whilst the kids were at school. About six months after my husband's departure and The Leader's death, we had arranged to meet one day. She sat me down and announced that she had something to tell me and that I would be upset.

What she then shared did indeed shock me to the core.

She proceeded to tell me that since The Leader's death, various members of the fellowship had started talking to one another – something he had discouraged strongly as "gossip". Gradually some truths had started to emerge, mostly from amongst the women. My friend then proceeded to tell me that she had actually been The Leader's mistress for several years and that it was transpiring that many of the women across the fellowship, ranging in age from teenage to sixties, both married and single, had also had sexual relationships with him.

What???? I felt sick to my stomach, and in some ways, it was more of a shock than when my husband had announced his intention to leave. We talked on, and she explained her place of repentance and subsequent confession to her husband. She asked me to forgive her for the deception. She explained that there was now crisis in the fellowship and there would be a fellowship meeting called shortly.

Good heavens. God, what is happening? Are you there?

And quickly my questions began to be…. Who else? Which of the women in our own little part of the fellowship? Why not me? How did I escape It? But I wouldn't have...... would I? But I wouldn't have thought any of the others would either. I loved my husband..... but didn't the other women also love their husbands? And what about the young single women? And where? And how? The man was blind! Never left his private room where he counselled people on his own with the door shut. The room I had been in on my own with him so many times.....

The questions kept coming and the shock kept reverberating. I felt traumatised. How could this have been?

And then, suddenly the light went on. It had not been right. It had never been right. There had been control. There had been manipulation. There had been deception. It had not been of God......

Not been of God? What had we done? What had I done? What had we got ourselves involved in?

How wrong had I been?

I worked through my memory and knew that I had never felt any attraction to him or felt any wrong vibes from him.

But I came to the place of realising that, had he not so suddenly and unexpectedly died, I would have been so, so vulnerable. An abandoned wife, a mother of two young children, emotionally beaten up and totally dependent on him for the roof over our heads; our security. Oh my. Would I have been so strong then? It was strange that in the last telephone call I had had with him, one in desperation when my husband had announced he was leaving, he seemed neither surprised nor particularly concerned. Did he have a plan?

I will never know the answer to that question. Nor will I ever know how well I would have stood up to the pressure, given my emotional brokenness and my instinctive needs to protect my children's wellbeing. I began to think of the women I knew so well who had been involved – and I learned a lesson. "There but for the grace of God go I "became truth to me and I realised that I needed to step back from judgement over those women who had been so compromised.

Shortly afterwards, a meeting was called for the whole fellowship. There was a totally heartrending, soul disturbing time of repentance; guilt-ridden women and shocked and traumatised men, and the fatally wounded fellowship was disbanded with the phrase of scripture ringing in our ears from John's gospel Chapter 8 *"Go, and sin no more"*. It would take some years and a big shift in cultural understanding to realise that these women had been subject to both sexual and spiritual abuse.

So, could it get any worse? It seems so, because now I had no husband, no income, no minister and no church fellowship! And I had no guarantee of a home for my children.

I, and a lot of people close to me, were confused. Where is God in all this? How would you ever trust a "man of God" again? For a while we continued to meet in our little house fellowship group, but I knew I needed more than that. But what? And where? There were some local joint church gatherings happening at the time, and I went to one and looked at the man on the platform and thought "How do I know you are what you say you are?"

Summer came round again, and it was a year since my husband had left. I heard from him only rarely, and received money rarely too, and on an ad hoc irregular basis. As I look back, I can't remember how we survived but we did. I sold my wedding, engagement and eternity rings that first Christmas and we got by. I would open the front door and find supermarket bags on the doorstep full of food. Things happened. With no other choice, I was trusting in the God I had learned about; and he truly showed Himself to know my need.

My parents lived locally, were retired and comfortably off. My father in particular had not taken the news of my husband's exit very well. Because he was hugely defensive of me? Well no! It was because he was ashamed and didn't want the wider family to know! It was the early 1980s and divorce was still socially unacceptable. I think my father also felt that it must have been my fault. He had been very fond of my husband and felt hurt and rejected himself but couldn't talk about it. Consequently, although they were certainly not hard up financially themselves, he never asked me if I was managing for money. My lovely mum would slip me a tenner out of her housekeeping once a month and dad never knew. I never heard from my brother, so there was no family support. But my God family were always there and through them and I think sometimes through angels, true to God's promise of being our Provider, there was indeed provision.

I was eventually told by the charitable trust that owned the house, that I could stay there indefinitely as long as I was fulfilling the stated criteria of the trust, which were: To help the poor and needy; To support the work of the Christian gospel in a locality. Well, I certainly fulfilled the poor and needy bit and if I settled in a church, maybe the second would be fulfilled.

It took a while to work through the doubts and suspicions, but eventually after a few months and some clear leading and direction from the Lord, we settled in a local Assemblies of

God Pentecostal church. The pastor there at the time was very kind and supportive and I began to feel safe.

Meanwhile, over the months since my husband had gone, I had not forgotten that summer week when I had actually been aware of the sense of a presence of the Lord which had brought me peace. Despite all the trauma of the end of the fellowship, I had not doubted Him, the truth of His existence, the truth of the fact that Jesus died for me and was my Saviour and friend, the truth of His word, and I was also aware of the ministry and gifts of His Holy Spirit, although my experience there was somewhat limited. I still had much to learn.

Afterthought: "No man is an island, entire of itself" John Donne wrote four hundred years ago. Human beings are intrinsically social creatures who need family and relationship. And yet loneliness is endemic in today's culture. Where did we go wrong?

Chapter 7: The beginning of recovery

"Light dawns in the darkness for the upright" Psalm 112 :4

And so another new chapter begins. The church that the three of us became part of was a small Assemblies of God Pentecostal church with a young and very dynamic minister. He was very kind and welcoming to my wounded little family. I was open with him and told him the whole sad story of my husband's desertion, my pastor's deception and my own overwhelming sense of failure and shame.

The fellowship that was, no longer met, and many of the relationships that both my children and I had come to love and depend on, were fragmenting, as people found their own way onwards from the shock and pain. It was the early 1980's and divorce statistics were rising but I, as a separated woman, was viewed with some suspicion by some church members and indeed in some other church denominations, I would not have been welcome at all. I was very sensitive to the prevailing mood and felt insecure, second class, tainted. A failure of a woman who couldn't keep a husband and was sometimes viewed by other married women as some sort of threat! I was once told that I needed to wear a hat to church as I didn't have a husband as my covering!!!

As the weeks went by, I began to ponder over that couple of years in the fellowship and my husband's irrational decision to leave. For a while I had thought maybe it was a consequence of the stress of the Brixton riots. I suppose I was thinking PTSD except I had never heard of that in 1981! But then I began to wonder exactly what his individual sessions with the Fellowship Leader had been about. It's the one thing we never discussed. We were very actively dissuaded from sharing "gossip" together and it was made clear that our private discussions with The Leader remained private. Some of the other members of our little fellowship had made contact with my husband on my behalf at the time of the big disclosure, thinking it might cause him to reconsider, but with no result. A long time later, my husband told me that he had missed us so much that he had deliberately started another relationship to ease the pain and was by then committed. I have never known exactly what pressure was exerted on him, but I do know The Leader was telling him that he couldn't be both a police officer and a Christian and he would need to choose!!! Outrageous! But I didn't know that at the time. I suspect there were also other pressures exerted to make him feel guilty and inadequate. Lord have mercy.

We were adjusting to life as a family of three – plus the dog! It was not easy! My daughter had always tended to be insecure and was very close to me. My son tended to deny any problems and lost himself in sport and his friendships as teenage years hit. I so remember the first time I had to go to a parents evening at his school – a boys' only environment which was completely alien to me as I had been to a girls' only school! I so struggled with the stigma of being a single parent (the early 80s remember!) and on this occasion, I had made contact with my husband and pleaded with him to come with me – to no avail, and in fact that encounter with him left me more bruised than ever.

I eventually began to feel accepted at church and started making some good friends. The church was growing, and our minister was a bit of a rising star in the denomination. He managed to grab many of the well-known speakers of the time whenever they were around London, and we had some amazing times with the building packed and people standing on the pavement outside to listen! I was getting involved and gaining confidence again in the God who I felt I had let down so badly by joining that fellowship. I struggled to accept the forgiveness I was taught I could receive. It seemed too easy.

My daughter was by now also in secondary school and life for me was mainly centred around being a Mum. I was still struggling to deal with my own deep pain, but I was also so aware of what hurt and damage these two men, their father and the Fellowship Leader had inflicted on their young lives and I felt guilty for not having protected them better.

As I just put one foot in front of the other day by day, I did begin to learn one very profound lesson. There is a battle to be won in my mind! I have always had a very active imagination. Perhaps I was just born that way, or perhaps it is the product of a comparatively lonely childhood, where my biggest pastime was reading. Whilst I was in Junior school, books were expensive (paperbacks had hardly been invented!) and were only available to me as birthday and Christmas presents, or from the local library. And in those days the libraries would only allow you to borrow one book at a time, so my perpetual cry during school holidays would be "Mum please can I have a penny for the bus fare to the library again?" I read most of Enid Blyton before moving on to Louisa M Alcott, Lorna Hill and many others. I lived each book in my imagination, and games with friends in the playground were always about us working out some imaginary scenario.

But now, my imagination was my enemy. I was tormenting myself with thoughts of my husband, where he was; who he was with; would he come back? what he was doing. And also my fears for the future; how would I survive? What would happen to me?

Do you remember the story of the scripture I found the night we had had an argument in Chapter 3? Well in the course of all the turmoil, I had remembered it.

15 *Perhaps the reason he was separated from you for a little while was that you might have him back forever— 16 no longer as a slave, but better than a slave, as a dear brother. He is very dear to me but even dearer to you, both as a fellow man and as a brother in the Lord.*

So, was that scripture a promise from God about the situation I now found myself in? Did it indeed mean my husband would come back?

And so my mind went round and round and with it my imagination taunted me with all sorts of images and scenarios. It became so bad it was like a TV programme I didn't want to watch but couldn't switch off. The noise in my head was too loud.

And then somehow, somewhere, I don't remember how, I came across the scripture in 2 Corinthians 10:5 which tells us to "take captive every thought to make it obedient to Christ". It was a revelation to me that I was in control of my mind, of what I thought about, of what was allowed to flash across the screen of my imagination. It had not occurred to me before. The saying "my mind ran away with me" was more how I assumed it all worked. My mind had a mind of its own so's to speak!

Anyway, this may be a true concept although its not an easy one. But somehow, I knew that if I was to cope without my husband; if I was to be what my children needed me to be, if I was to stay sane, I had to grasp this.

I had also begun at this time to really grasp the concept of the presence of God being with me at all times and was trying to practise that. I would therefore lose count of how many times during a normal day I would silently or out loud ask God to help me, Jesus to be with me, and often would run upstairs in desperation to the bedroom, throw myself to my knees at the end of the bed, bang my head on the duvet and ask the Lord to take these thoughts from me. Nothing dramatic happened, it continued to be a battle for my mind, but gradually over the following months, nay years, my internal world gradually became quieter, healthier and a lot more peaceful.

Anyway, back to the kids. It felt to me like I was being fought over. The evenings seemed to be a constant battle between the kids for my attention. And I frequently seemed to feel that I was being torn in half!! It was "Mum, can you help me with my German homework?" to "Mum, I thought you were going to help my with my art" and "Mum, I need you to help with my flute practise"; "Mum I need to talk to you"!! It seemed were in competition for my undivided attention, and whilst I did understand the need behind that, it was stressful for me.

I happened to mention it to our Minister one day and his response was to ask me whether I'd consider taking in a lodger!! My first response was: I don't need someone else to look after! But he went on to explain that I had a spare room, it would help my non-existent budget; it would fulfil the Trust's criteria and might provide a bit of a buffer to the intense relationships we were experiencing as a family unit. Hmmm. I said I would think about it. I didn't really. And about a week later my minister rang me from his office. It was a life changing phone call.

"I have a young lady in my office who is homeless. Her father has thrown her out of home. She plans to get a flat with her older sister in the next few weeks but meanwhile has nowhere to go. She is seventeen, clean and well presented. What do you think?"

What did I think? I hadn't a clue, but he was the Minister, and I didn't feel I could say "No!"

I talked to the kids, and the next day Penny arrived and moved into the spare room. A friend had dropped her off and all her "luggage" was in black plastic sacks. It transpired that Penny was the second of a family of five. Their mother had without any warning dropped dead in their bathroom of a brain tumour about two years previously. They were living on a (fairly) local estate which had a pretty bad reputation, and I gradually came to understand that, however Dad might have coped before his wife's death, he most certainly was not able to cope now. Penny was working evenings at a not so local Greek restaurant and would come and go at all sorts of times, bringing lots of Halloumi cheese home with her and leaving it stuck all over the grill pan!!

She was open and chatty and amenable and gradually her life began to shape itself around our family rhythms. She asked lots of questions! She wanted to know where my husband was, and then why he had gone, and probably the most important question was "Why do you go to church every Sunday?" And after my inadequate explanation; "Can I come as well?"

And so she did. And she heard about Jesus and chose to surrender her life to him, and she threw herself into the youth group at church and she very shortly afterwards decided to be baptised. She proposed asking all her family to the baptism and asked if they could come back home afterwards for a cup of tea and a sandwich.

The evening of her baptism the church was packed as usual, and all the family were late. By the time they arrived, the seats that had been saved for them had been relinquished and they ended up in random seats here and there and I found I had Susie, the 13-year-old sister, on my lap!! The service was great, several people including Penny were baptised, and after the service we all arrived home and I was kept busy making teas and coffees and passing round sandwiches and cakes for about 20 people! Young Susie hardly left my side and at one point stated that she would like to be baptised like Penny and please, could she? I explained that there was a bit more to it than that, and that she needed to learn about Jesus and maybe be a bit older. Then I felt some sort of nudge from somewhere and found myself suggesting that she might like to come for the weekend to come to church and learn some more.

And so began yet another unexpected turn of events.

Afterthought: Viktor Frankl the Austrian psychologist and holocaust survivor is quoted as saying "Everything can be taken from a man, but the last of the human freedoms: to choose one's attitude in any given set of circumstances". This a profound life lesson. We have the power of choice over our thoughts but we so often allow our thoughts to lead to destructive behaviours rather than positive ones.

Chapter 8: Extended family

"Do not forget to show hospitality to strangers, for by so doing some people have shown hospitality to angels without knowing it! Hebrews 13:2

Let's stop here for a while on my journey so that I can tell you the story of Susie – and others!

From the time of her sister's baptism, Susie started to come and stay roughly every other weekend. She was just a year older than my daughter and they got on well together. That first weekend that she came to stay, I had arranged to go and pick her up from outside her address at two o'clock on Saturday. I found the right place but two o'clock, quarter past two came and went and no signs of Susie. (Remember it's still the 80s – no mobile phones!) So, I left the car and found the right set of steps and then the right front door and knocked. A flustered Susie answered and apologised saying she was just packing and inviting me in. I am tempted to describe for you in detail the circumstances in which this broken family was living but it is right to honour the feelings and memories of those involved and for that reason the details are omitted.

Suffice it to say, it was not just about general disorder and chaos in practical terms, but it was also evident that the adult in the home had abdicated responsibility and the boundaries most parents would ensure were in place to protect and safeguard their children were woefully absent. I was shocked rigid with what I saw but I kept my reactions under wraps and we went back to my place.

I kept my reactions under wraps and Susie got her stuff together and we went back to my place. When we arrived, I got Susie settled doing things with my daughter and went up to my room and wept. Wept with shock and grief for what this child was living with. I was aware of struggling with feelings of anger towards the father and anxiety about what I should do. I actually rang our minister and downloaded. There were very few other people who ever knew exactly what Susie was living with.

From then on Susie was a regular weekend visitor and more depending on school holidays etc. She was loved and nurtured and the church was amazing at helping me provide for her. In those early days, I took her out to buy shoes to replace the ones she wore with holes in the soles, I bought her bras which she needed but only had her sister's castoffs. And the church bought her a much-needed winter coat as the weather got colder. She was also included in church youth activities and whenever there was a cost involved it was found from somewhere.

I gradually got to know the whole family. Over a long period of time, I concluded that their Mum had been a loving and nurturing mother, laying a good foundation in her children's lives despite what must have been financial hardship and despite what I know was not an easy marriage. Her sudden and dramatic death had a huge impact on them all in different ways. Susie was loving and kind, biddable, eager to learn, responsive, unselfconscious - and at times really exasperating. Her concentration was poor, and she struggled with any aspect of organisation and in a nutshell, like her sister Penny she would affectionately be referred to as "scatty". But they were now both part of the family albeit Susie was a commuting member until she left school at 16.

Into this mix, my minister made another phone call to me one day. Some contacts of his had a daughter about to start an accountancy training in Sutton, did he know of any family that had a spare room and could put her up for a bit whilst she found her feet! And so, after discussions with Penny, who was totally amenable, Margo moved in to share her room and we became a family of five and at weekends six (plus two dogs!)

Penny and Margo could not have been more different. Margo was studious, highly organised, came from a solid Christian family background and was very focussed. Penny took life as it came, was anything but organised, was learning and growing in her Christian faith and cheerfully outgoing. But it worked! They shared a room for eighteen months or so and grew to love and respect each other and tolerate the bits that annoyed them! Margo was able to move on to her own flat and went on to become a partner in the accountancy firm to which she was articled.

Penny didn't stay long at the Greek restaurant and got an office job working literally down the road. She eventually fell in love with a young man in our church and eventually married him and went on to have three lovely daughters. I did the catering for their wedding reception, which to this day remains the biggest hospitality challenge I have ever undertaken!

Meanwhile, just as Susie was preparing for her O level exams, her father took her and her younger brother and overnight and without warning did a runner from their home to his elderly mother-in-law's flat in East London to escape creditors. Susie and her brother were uprooted from their schools and relocated with no advance warning and no means of letting anybody know. For a while we didn't know where Susie was, which was very distressing until eventually she was able to get to a phone box. During that period of time, Susie turned up on the doorstep one midweek afternoon when she should have been at school and said she had run away. It was really hard to tell her she couldn't stay, that the law wouldn't allow it – until she was sixteen, and then she could legally leave home. When that time came, I needed to have conversations with both my kids.

My daughter admitted that much as she loved Susie, she was not ready for her to move in, because she was not ready to share her mum on a permanent basis. She had been going through some emotional growing up pains and we talked and prayed for her situations together regularly. Surprisingly, her brother expressed strongly that we should make room for Susie – but they were both at a stage when they contradicted and goaded each other at any opportunity – the joys of parenting teenagers!

Susie moved in with a young couple in church for about a year until my daughter came down from her room one evening and told me that she had been praying and that she felt God had spoken to her through a scripture and it was time for Susie to move in. So, at last she did.

By this time our church had a very large youth group, and our home was a frequent venue for youth gatherings. It was quite normal to have twenty or thirty teenagers in the house consuming quantities of whatever I could make available.

One of these young men was Danny, who had been on the point of being expelled from school, when a group of young Americans hosted by our church, turned up at his school and introduced him to Jesus. His life was turned around and he was a part of this group of kids in my home. Then his girlfriend whom he'd met at college, started turning up at weekends too and started to get to know the girls including my daughter and Susie. Anna commuted quite a way to join us each weekend, and yes, you've guessed it, eventually she moved in too! She shared a room with Susie, and Penny having by now got married, we were once again a family of five.

It was a warm and rewarding time! At a season of life when I could have been forced inward, struggling with so many negative emotions, I was forced to be put myself aside on a regular basis for these youngsters and it was good. What is it about that generation that they so often come alive and are ready to talk round about bedtime? I can remember one evening when a conversation started between four of us; my daughter, Susie and Anna and I . Somehow, we all ended up sitting on the stairs and there we stayed into the early hours. It was good for me too, to be on the receiving end of their questions about life and particularly faith. It caused me to think through, not just that I believed in the God of the Bible, but why and how I believed. My son was beginning to question faith and some of his questions were tough.

So, it was a rich time. An exhausting time, young people coming and going, washing, cooking, three different sounds of music coming out of three different bedrooms, providing lifts here there and everywhere. Most parents of teenagers will be familiar with this and ultimately, I was forced to lay down some house rules to share some of the chores.

Again, it took me a long time to be able to realise the extent to which their mother's tragic death had affected Susie but with hindsight I gradually understood that when I met her, she was basically suffering some sort of post-traumatic stress. I think the trauma of her mother's death in their own home, and a total lack of any kind of external support let alone suitable bereavement counselling had left its mark. Her father was also dealing with bereavement and, I suspect, had always left parenting to his wife so was unable to begin to meeting his children's needs. I often wonder if Penny & Susie had not happened across the love and security of the family of God, whether their lives would have been irretrievably damaged.

Sometime in the middle of all this, I can't remember which year, I was on my way to church one midweek evening to a meeting that was not actually one led by our church. As I walked into the building, I was vaguely aware of a young-looking couple loitering on the path, but I was with someone else and ignored them. As I got into the building, I was hit from nowhere with a sense of guilt – I had ignored them – I shouldn't have done. So, I went back and spoke with them. It transpired that they were called Steve & Georgie; they were homeless, she was pregnant, they had been sleeping in a local churchyard and Social Services had suggested that they should come to our church for help so they were looking for the Minister. I became aware of this silent, but loud voice in my head quoting words I recognised "I was hungry, and you fed me, I was naked, and you clothed me, I was thirsty and you gave me something to drink". ** I knew they were words spoken by Jesus – and they wouldn't go away. I had been joined by another couple I knew by this time who had also been going into the building for a meeting and had stopped with me. I explained that the Minister wouldn't be there that evening, and we suggested the young couple came inside, and my friend's husband went to get some fish and chips, Meanwhile, I phoned our Minister from the church office to ask what to do to be told that I should tell them to go back to Social Services in the morning!

It was one of those moments when you teeter fleetingly between two decisions. In a few split seconds I realised I was choosing between the sensible decision of the world and the risky decision of faith. It was agreed that the lad, Steve, would go home for the night with my friends and that the girl, Georgie, would come home with me, and they could go to Social Services in the morning. They protested about being split up, but we stuck to our guns and they accepted.

On the way home in the car, I had a brief panic, thinking what have I done! My two children are at home, Penny would have to share her room, and I knew nothing about the truth of this girl! She could abscond in the night with the family silver (that is a figure of speech because there was no silver!) or worse. Penny being Penny didn't bat an eyelid when I arrived home with this dishevelled girl and she quickly sorted out a spare nightie, some bubble bath and a towel, whilst I made up the spare bed. (It was in the brief period between Margo leaving and Anna arriving).

As I went to bed that night praying that I hadn't done something irresponsible, I felt that maybe, maybe, God was asking me if I was willing to give her six weeks of my life.

Just six weeks. My sort of conditional response was, well let's see if we're all still alive and in one piece by the morning!

Of course we were, and I soon realised that Georgie was exhausted from sleeping rough, undernourished – although she quickly confessed that she wasn't really pregnant; that was a ploy to evoke concern - and that she came from Cornwall and had an 18 month old son whom she had abandoned to her parents. Steve stayed with my friends for a few days and would visit, but he was more rebellious; their relationship was stormy (my son and I had to break up a couple of fights involving smashed glass and threats) and after a few days, he disappeared from the neighbourhood, never to be heard of again. But Georgie stayed. She began to relax. She developed a severe abscess under a tooth, so there were trips backwards and forwards to my dentist, and she began asking questions about our home; why Penny lived with us; where my husband was; and why we went to church. There were long chat sessions with Penny in their bedroom and she came to church with us the following Sunday. Over a short period this young girl – she was 19 – began to unfold from a taut, tense young woman, self-defensive, and slightly aggressive, to a young woman flowering into adulthood and an acceptance of responsibility. She met the person of Jesus and accepted that he had died for her. Meanwhile I would quietly talk about her little boy back at home and how much he needed his mum, and she knew she had to go back. Our church arranged a special, unscheduled baptismal service just for Georgie, and I drove her up to Victoria coach station and put her on a coach home to Cornwall exactly six weeks after I met her.

The strange end to this particular story is that I never saw or heard from Georgie again! A few years later, some friends from church were on holiday in Cornwall near where she came from and found she was indeed there, with her little boy, a member of a local church. Otherwise, I think I would have suspected that we actually had hosted an angel!

The years marched on as they do, and everyone grew up a bit – including me! Penny was married. Margo married a young man from church and the two of them have raised their son in church too, Anna was with me until she and Danny got married and I haven't mentioned Hilary who was the youngest daughter of dear friends who went off to Greece to live for a few years and at seventeen years old, Hilary didn't want to uproot and go with them, so she came to live with us. It was a tough one, because it wasn't really her choice and understandably, she resented the situation. It was only possible because by this time my precious daughter had at 19 years old married and moved to Yorkshire, and my lovely son had also left home. That left me for a couple of years with three very special surrogate daughters, they all got on well together, helping each other deal with growing up and teaching me a lot in the process.

Anna & Danny got married, had three children and still live locally; Hilary's parents came home just before her wedding and she was with me until then. She and her husband and children now live in Australia. And Susie......... well she was the last to leave the nest. She was on holiday in Greece when she met a nice young man from New Zealand who was "doing Europe". They deliberated long and hard about whether to settle in New Zealand or the UK and eventually got married in the UK and settled in New Zealand. I am so proud of Susie. She found settling in New Zealand challenging. She missed her close girlfriends and wider family enormously. But she and her lovely husband have made it work and they have kept practising their faith, have raised three strong sons, run a very successful business, have a beautiful house with acres of ground near the waterfront and now the boys are grown, often fly off for a weekend in their own small aircraft to visit the other New Zealand island or even Australia!

A true Cinderella story really – except featuring a redeeming Saviour instead of a fairy Godmother.

Afterthought: "Hospitality means primarily the creation of free space where the stranger can enter and become a friend instead of an enemy. Hospitality is not to change people, but to offer them space where change can take place. It is not to bring men and women over to our side, but to offer freedom not disturbed by dividing lines." Henri Nouwen

Chapter 9: Endings…..and beginnings

"God is our refuge and strength in times of trouble" (Psalm 46:1)

Life as a single parent was tough. Ever since the stressful events on my sons twelfth birthday, both the children had refused to see their father. They couldn't recognise the man who had been causing such disturbance on that night; trust had been damaged and consequently we had very little contact. Occasionally I had a phone call, occasionally some money would show up, but it was as though the supportive, reliable, responsible husband I had shared life with had simply disappeared. By now, I knew he was living in a flat locally with another woman, a policewoman from his station. But I still kept that scripture at the back of my mind "perhaps the reason why he was separated from you for a little while was that you might have him back".

Two years had somehow gone by when a brown envelope dropped unannounced through the letter box which turned out to contain a solicitor's letter inviting me to divorce my husband on the grounds of his admitted adultery.

I suppose it could be said that I should have been expecting it. But I wasn't and I was truly shocked. Was he serious? Our long courtship; our marriage; all the memories, the secrets we'd shared, the birth of each of our children…….. to be ended in a court of law? No!

My instinctive choice was to ignore the letter. He might still change his mind. But reason prevailed and I knew I couldn't ignore it. But I was being offered a choice, and invitation to divorce him and everything in me did not want that, did not want to be the instigator of the end of the contract I had made and kept. Apart from which, at that time, and I have re-thought this since, I thought that God did not approve of divorce. So, I replied accordingly that I did not choose to divorce my husband.

Consequently, a couple of weeks later, another brown envelope arrived containing the petition for divorce instigated by my husband to divorce me. The grounds stated were interesting. The only charges against me as the case for divorce were based entirely on my choice to become a Christian and the subsequent actions arising from that choice.

It was time to see a solicitor myself. I was truly indignant! How could I be divorced for being a Christian! I had potentially dozens of witnesses who could testify that he had made the same decision and taken the same choices!!

I voiced my indignation to the man behind the desk and mentioned the legion of witnesses I could produce in the solicitor's office and his reply has echoed in my memory ever since! " I regret to tell you Mrs Sullivan, that if you did that you would simply prove to the judge that your relationship is irretrievably broken down "

A friend came with me to the divorce court for the decree nisi. I bought a new dress to wear. It was red. I think it was an expression of protest. She and I sat together in the courtroom and heard a whole long list of couples' names read out and at the sound of the gavel on wood, all those marriages were declared over. All those engagement celebrations, wedding days, honeymoons over. All that togetherness of planning, anticipation, home making, baby birthing, parenting, over.

However, our names were called, and it was explained that the two of us were required to go before the judge about our children. I had prayed about this so much…. "please, please God, don't let him contend access. Please Lord protect the children, please don't let them be forced into arrangements they don't want. Please Lord God, Heavenly Father, please give me wisdom in this". We had avoided each other in the main courtroom, but there was no escaping now and we stood side by side in front of a judge in a small side room. The judge was kind and gentle. He stated that he understood that the children had not seen their father in almost two years and asked me why this was. I explained. He nodded and then very kindly explained that he was going to rule that their father should be able to see them for two hours on a Sunday afternoon once a month, on the understanding that he should not take them back to the home that he was currently sharing with a young woman.

I was so relieved and thanked God for hearing my prayers. I knew without doubt that the children needed a relationship with their dad, and I wanted that for them, of course I did. But I knew they needed time to accommodate the huge shock of the change. And I also knew that to find their dad living with a young woman only seven years older than our son was something that would require huge adjustment and I was so grateful to the Judge for having that sensitivity and knew that my prayers had been heard and answered.

And so it was. My marriage was apparently over. I am single. A divorced woman. Just like that.

The first couple of times my now ex-husband collected them, I was on tenterhooks until he brought them back, but gradually confidence grew all round and when just a few weeks later after the decree absolute, he remarried, the children were easier with the situation and eventually began to visit his home and get to know their stepmother. It was right for them. It was so, so hard for me.

Gradually, as he would bring the children back after a visit and they would go straight up to bed, he would sometimes stay, and we would talk. Talk about the kids, and gradually talk about us. Such bittersweet conversations at times. I listened to him telling me it was never my fault; that after he'd left, he was so lonely; missed us so much, he knew he would have to get married again. It was clear there had been pressure from the Fellowship Leader but he was never able to articulate exactly what that was. Obviously, he was no longer practising his faith and to some extent blamed God for what had happened. So reassuring to hear in some ways but heartbreaking in others. I would show him out of the front door and sit and sob. And what about the promise I thought I had from God? I didn't know. I prayed, I said sorry to God if I got that wrong, but I never lost the sense that it was a promise and I "hid it in my heart". (Luke 2:19)

That year was a really tough one. The week the divorce was finalised, I had to take the decision to have our precious dog, Seamus, a beautiful Irish Setter, put to sleep. He was 14 years old and struggling to walk and at roughly six stone in weight, I couldn't carry him. The children had never known life without him and over a long period of time, I had deliberately tried to prepare them by talking about how when we eventually lost him, we would have another puppy straight away, Lack of funds meant that I had been taking him to the PDSA clinic rather than the local vet. I do not believe in allowing animals to suffer to spare our own grief, so on the day I had decided it was time, I prepared myself, saw the kids off to school, got Seamus in the car and drove to the clinic. I had once taken my brother's dog to the vet to be put down because they couldn't face it, so I knew what to expect. When it was our turn, I explained to the PDSA vet that I had decided it was time. He agreed and proceeded to try and take the dog's lead from me. "No", I protested, "I will stay with him! I'm not leaving him". The vet was adamant that I could not stay with my dog. He assured me that he would not be left alone, that it would be done straight away, but that I had to leave him. Otherwise, they would refuse to take him, and I would have to take him elsewhere. I was devastated. There are tears in my eyes as I type this 40 years later. Seamus was a loyal member of the family. My son had learned to stand by pulling himself up hanging on to Seamus. (He'd also learned to drop unwanted food from his highchair to the dog strategically positioned below!) He had been our constant companion on hundreds of miles of walks. He had so helped my loneliness by being a constantly available cuddle. And I was expected to betray all that by leaving him to die with no one he loved beside him. However, I had no money for a private vet; I had no reasonable choice. I sobbed as I left him and all that day.

The next day, a Saturday, my mum had been a bit poorly, so I popped over in the morning to see her. I sat on her bed and we both cried together about Seamus, and then something was said, I can't remember what, but it made us both laugh. I only stayed about 40 minutes, because I'd left my son at home on his own – my daughter was out with her cousins.

Later that afternoon, I popped over to my brother's to pick her up and as they opened the front door to me, their phone rang. My brother answered it. We all fell silent standing together in the hall as we heard his response. Clearly bad news? It was my father on the phone in a state. My mother had just collapsed and died in their living room.

It's the one and only time in my life that a scream has involuntarily come out of my mouth, and I remember it was followed by me crying out "No! No more! I can't take any more"! A dead marriage, a dead dog and a dead mother all in a matter of months. And my protest was levelled at God. For probably the first time since I had met Him 14 years before, I briefly doubted – not His existence, but His benevolence. And I was angry and felt unjustly treated!

However, there was no time for self-indulgence. My brother and I rushed over to my parents' house to find my father distraught and my mother's body on the sofa where she had died. So, there were things to sort out, my dad to take care of, my two children to console, not only about their very much-loved Nana, but also the loss of their canine companion the day before. And I remembered my promise about getting a puppy straight away! Oh, Lord, how am I going to do that?

The next day, the children spent the day with friends, and I knew as I went to pick them up on the afternoon, that we would be passing an RSPCA kennels locally. I pondered going in to see if they had any puppies that needed a home. As I was leaving our friend' s house with the children, my friend pressed a brown envelope into my hand which I put in my handbag. I had no idea what it was but vaguely though it was something she didn't want the children to see so left it for later to investigate. On the spur of the moment, we called in at the RSPCA and I silently prayed that we would choose the right dog – I imagined loads of puppies awaiting forever homes. They had just two puppies available to view. They were both of indiscriminate parentage and were what was left of an abandoned litter. One, the female, was mainly white with some brown & black markings; the other was a black male with some brown. They were both delightful. What puppy isn't! The children were rather favouring the white one, although I was somewhat reluctant to have a bitch. Then the kennel maid appeared and explained the costs involved. Costs? I had naively thought that needy puppies went to caring homes free of charge!!

She further explained that the costs were to cover initial inoculations, which they both had, provision of a collar and lead which was compulsory and for the bitch an extra amount to cover her being brought back to be spayed. Oh no. I had two- or three-pounds cash on me and virtually nothing in the bank. The little white bitch would therefore cost £18 and the little black boy was £12.50. I braced myself to say that we would have to leave it to another day, explaining quietly to the children that I didn't have enough money. My daughter immediately said "What was in that brown envelope you put in your handbag?". I hesitated then took the envelope out of my bag and opened it. It contained a £10 note. I turned out my purse that contained £ 2. 74!

So we went home that night with a new member of the family. And we called him Toby, which means "God is good".

Toby turned out to be a very frail little puppy. I suspect he was actually younger than the RSPCA had estimated he was, and his digestive system really still needed his mother's milk. On the day of my mother's funeral, two very precious friends stayed with him all day, because he was so poorly. They later told me they had prayed over him all day because they felt as a family we would not cope with another tragedy. Toby survived and grew but not a lot! I was told he was probably a collie cross, but he certainly didn't grow into collie size inheritance! But he was the most gentle loving boy; intelligent and obedient and so, so sensitive to people. But he was only a half pint in size and I missed my big dog, so one night dropping off one of the children's friends, she said "My dog's just had puppies do you want to come and see?" Well, of course I did….. and the rest is history. A few weeks later, a little brown mongrel joined us whom we called Bruno, (actually after the handsome young pianist in "Fame" on the TV!!) but very appropriately because of his colour! Bruno was absolutely devoted to me in particular. He was an insecure little chap and followed me everywhere. The two dogs were devoted to each other although Toby was always

Top Dog and was followed dutifully around by a devoted Bruno!

Meanwhile, life was busy; two teenage children; an extended household; increasing involvement in church. Divorce had brought with it a financial settlement at last, which relieved some of the pressure, but money was, and remained, a stressful factor.

Speaking of church, I had got quite friendly with the minister's wife. It's quite challenging being married to a busy minister, and I sought to be some support to her where I could. She ran the regular ladies' meetings in church and actually hated having to be on the platform, so I started to help her out undertaking some of the platform tasks, doing introductions and notices etc. The church was going really well, but after we'd been there less than a couple of years, I noticed that my friend was more than usually stressed, in fact seemed really troubled and indicated that there was something going on that she couldn't talk about but asked me to pray for her.

Eventually the truth came out. Our lovely, charismatic, highly thought of young minister was having an affair with his secretary.

Unbelievable. On a church level it was devastation. Hurt, bewildered, disillusioned people - again- and two broken families. On a personal level, this was the second "man of God" to fall in front of me in two years. Another devastating betrayal of trust. And for my now coming up to fifteen-year-old son, another example of Christian men falling short, and it would seem for him the beginning of the end of belief in God and commitment to church. The minister left, was replaced and we soldiered on.

I began to be very stirred about the role and place of women. It seemed to me that Jesus himself was almost revolutionary in the attention and space he made for the women around him. And yet the church seemed to have boundaries around what women were permitted to do. They could be entrusted to teach and influence children in Sunday school, and they could go and risk their lives in foreign countries as missionaries but had to wear hats and not be in leadership within many of our churches. I began to read my bible with this in mind and venture out a little bit in taking some lead in women's meetings and meanwhile I was also pushing ahead to try and learn what prayer really should look like.

Some close friends at the time were involved with some of the Afro Caribbean churches springing up around our part of London and I visited with them on occasion. In the mid-80s they had a Nigerian Bishop staying with them who was visiting the area. I had met him briefly and was surprised when I was told he wanted to see me. We arranged a meeting when he told me that the Lord had given him a dream about me that he wanted to share. He had dreamed of a bird who lived in a cage. This bird had water and food in the cage, and every so often it would sing a song. But one day, the cage door opened, and the bird flew out and flew down to a field of millet where it fed and fed and fed. Then it flew to the top of the tallest tree in the forest and sang a song it had never sung before. "Does this mean anything to you?" he asked. I pondered. "Yes", I said, "I think I'm definitely the bird". "So", he asked "What is the cage, Wendy? "

I thought and duly replied that I thought it was my living circumstances at home; teenage children, extended family, big house to run, limited finance etc. He nodded wisely and just replied "Well, you need to ask the Lord about that". And that was that - for then.

Time had gone by, and my ex-husband and his wife had had their first child, which altered the financial settlement, and I was going to have to face getting a job. I hadn't worked outside of the home for seventeen years. I had no idea what I wanted to do, or indeed what I could do! But needs must.

Afterthought: "Let your hopes not your hurts define your future". Robert H. Schuller

Chapter 10: Career Girl (1)

"Never be lacking in zeal but keep your spiritual fervour serving the Lord" Romans 12:11

I had not had a regular job for seventeen years and had no idea what to look for or what I could cope with. I decided to work part time to start with as both the children were still at school, and it preferably needed to be local. I applied fairly randomly for four jobs, one in a doctor's surgery, one in a building society, one for the Civil Aviation Authority and one for an organisation called Crown Agents about which I didn't know much! I was offered three out of four jobs (the one I thought I really wanted, which was working for the Civil Aviation Authority, was the one I didn't get!). After much heart searching, and a little prayer, I decide to take the Crown Agent's offer and in late 1987 I duly started working five six-hour days a week as an Buying Assistant. There turned out to be two distinct advantages to this offer that I gave no consideration to at all before accepting it. One was that I would eventually work flexi hours, and the other was that they ran a non-contributory pension scheme.

It transpired that I was working as an Assistant Buyer for the island of St Helena which is in the middle of the Atlantic Ocean.

Crown Agents was originally part of the Foreign and Commonwealth Office of the British Government set up in the 1800's when Britain was at its colonial height and it was the department that handled all the procurement and shipping requirements for those colonies. That meant CA were buying and shipping anything from furniture and dinner services for the Governor's Residences to foodstuffs, building materials and in time vehicles and engineering equipment,

St Helena was at that time, the most remote island in the world. It is in the South Atlantic a third of the way between the coast of West Africa and the coast of S America and at 410 square kilometres it is twice the size of Washington DC. It had no airport because of its rocky terrain (one was eventually opened in 2016 but with restrictions on the size of aircraft that can safely land). It had no airfield, no political parties, no cows, and is populated by people from both European and African descent who were originally shipwrecked on the slave trade route. There was a British garrison established on the island in the 17th century and Napoleon Bonaparte died there in exile. Students who were leaving the island for university places in the UK were shown videos to teach them about trains, stations, lifts, escalators, ATMs etc. Fascinating place.

St Helena's only contact with the outside world was the RMS St Helena which did the round trip from Bristol via Cape Town and then Ascension Island once every 6 weeks or so. The capital Jamestown was the only port. All the goods we ordered on their behalf e.g. wheat, maize, evaporated milk and cars were shipped from Bristol or loaded at Cape Town and when CA staff visited our client there, they flew to Cape Town and then boarded the RMS for the rest of the journey.

I gradually learned all this, along with the understanding that a Buying Assistant took care of the orders the Buyer had placed and in contact with the various suppliers made sure each consignment was delivered correctly and on time for being loaded onto the boat. It was interesting work, and I gradually got the hang of it. Over the next three years, I went on to work as the Buying Assistant for Hong King, and then Fiji and the South Pacific islands.

Eventually I was promoted to Buyer, but by then the system had changed and so instead of buying for a geographical location, I was buying computers for anywhere in the world!!

Times change and the former colonial nations changed as they became independent. They took over procurement for themselves but now increasingly needed technical advice on a consultancy basis and so Crown Agents business diversified and I moved over to our Consultancy business to work on the management of projects financed by the international donor community. That's when my travelling adventures began.

My first trip to Africa in 1994 took in Zambia. Mozambique and South Africa. I will never forget coming out of the airport in Lusaka, Zambia and seeing the red soil of Africa for the first time. I was immediately reminded of the Genesis story and the creation of Adam in the garden of Eden, which was thought to have been located in the area of Ethiopia. The name Adam is sometimes translated as "son of the red earth". So special.

I loved Africa although it brought me face to face with the realities of international aid and its pitfalls for the first time. One of the blessings of this job was that I was able to feel that in some way CA was making a difference. Britain at that time was near the top of the league table of nations that gave to the development of third world nations along with the Japanese and the EU. CA were at the forefront of delivering British Government aid in Disaster and Emergency situations. We were frequently first on the ground with emergency equipment after earthquakes, volcanoes and hurricanes. We had a huge medical expertise delivering vaccination programmes, hygiene and birth control programmes and goods in many of the remote areas of the world.

But it had its downside. In Zambia, we were visiting a large and ongoing medical project financed by the British Government. As part of that we flew from Lusaka in a twelve-seater plane up to the Copperbelt in the North of the country and to the towns of Kitwe and Ndola. As we flew we passed over rural villages with their round mud and grass structure huts, before landing in the busy copper mining town of Kitwe where we were visiting the local hospital which had been built, along with one in Ndola, forty miles away, as parting gifts from Britain when Zambia (formerly Northern Rhodesia) became independent from Britain in 1964. They were built on the model of a then state of the art hospital just built in Glasgow – as I found out, even to the installation of a central heating plant – in a sub-tropical country! The problem was that there had been no provision made for ongoing maintenance, so as we were taken on a tour of this large hospital, we found that a huge percentage of the windows were broken, out of the three X-ray rooms that had been fully equipped and functional, only one machine in one of the rooms still worked and that only because an ingenious Zambian engineer had plundered other broken down machines of parts in order to keep one machine functioning. There was no budget for maintenance and no ready supply of spares in country and so everything had or was falling into disrepair and non-function. Families of patients camped out in the grounds, and there was a heart-rending moment for me when we went to the children's wards and found rows of cots with just a couple of feet between them, and each cot had a small bundle of humanity lying there and each cot had a mother standing and watching over it. Mothers are mothers all over the world.

From the travesty of this hospital facility we were then taken for lunch to the British project manager's house for lunch, and not for the last time during my overseas visits, I was confused and hurt and offended as we sat down to a wonderful lunch with crystal glasses and designer cutlery and flown in food, all in a beautiful bungalow surrounded by lush green manicured lawns that shone like velvet in the bright sunlight. No. My heart was troubled. "Love your neighbour as yourself" ** What does that really look like?

That was my first visit to Zambia but not my last. I loved Mozambique with its Portuguese inheritance buildings and azure sea, and South Africa, both Johannesburg and Durban. Over the next few years, I found myself in Pakistan managing our office in Islamabad whilst the local office manager was on leave. It was my first experience of travelling on my own as a woman in a Muslim country. I was treated with great respect (except when I was temporarily kidnapped by a taxi driver in Lahore who wouldn't take me where I wanted to go!), and again I struggled with the contrast between the at best simple life and at worst life of acute poverty that the majority of people lived; the chaotic hubbub on the streets of Faisalabad as colourfully decorated lorries juggled their way between dozens of heavily laden bicycles, donkeys and even camels, whilst cows wandered freely amongst it all. And then the superb beauty and calm of my hotel, owned by the Agha Khan and sporting furniture inlaid with gold and set up a long drive in an oasis of calm that bore no resemblance to the bustle of the town around it.

Bangladesh was different. I didn't stay in a luxury hotel in Dhaka but in the British Aid Guest House Association Club (known as the BAGHA!). Below is an extract from my journal written in December 2001.

My first comment is probably one of regret that I didn't really get out of Dhaka – I would love to see something of rural Bangladesh – both to the North and the South – I'm not really a city person at the best of times – and I would not be able to rate Dhaka as one of my favourite cities that is for sure. At the same time – its not easy just to take off into rural Bangladesh – not for me anyway. I would need a guide / driver and someone to go with – I don't think I'm brave enough to go on my own.

The overriding thing about Dhaka is the traffic –and its resulting pollution. I do not think I could live with it. The weather has been clear and dry with temperatures hovering above 80 degrees – and yet one's impression is not of blue tropical skies – but just of greyness because the extent of the traffic pollution is so bad. The city is therefore very dirty. It is actually very well supplied with lovely trees and tropical vegetation everywhere – but many of them are literally brown - covered with the deposits of pollution from the traffic.

Added to that the streets are liberally scattered with rubbish – piles of it on street corners – or anywhere really. It is often covered with large scavenger birds – rooks probably, the occasional dog or even more occasional cat, and quite frequently very small children picking it over to see what they can find. Everything looks as though it has seen better days.

Of the hundreds of thousands of three wheeled bicycle rickshaws, a few are new and shiny and the bright decorations are still bright. In the main they are old and worn and run down with the colours faded and the decorations limp and tattered. Every view you look at is seen through the haze of pollution. Today we passed the military and air force establishments, which had actual planes mounted outside. But the planes were not silver metal or green painted – they were brown – covered in a thick layer of dust.

The new city has been well designed with long straight and wide roads. Totally unable, even so, to cope with the volume of traffic – 80% of which is made up of rickshaws and" baby taxis" and only the balance of cars – very few lorries and buses. The traffic and business of the streets is not just comprised of vehicles, but also pedestrians – there are thousands. And in all of this, there is no sense of order, discipline, rules – its every man and vehicle for itself – and if you have a horn, then sound it all the time! There are occasional sets of traffic lights at really large junctions – where a roundabout wouldn't have fitted – but I didn't see any of them working. Wherever traffic forms queues, then beggars, men, women and children appear at the car windows, tapping on them and staring inside. They're not aggressive and never attempt to open the car door but it is very disturbing and distressing.

Some of the beggars are in a pretty bad way. Their weapon of choice here is acid which is easily available and there are a lot of acid attacks in Bangladesh. Apparently, men will punish their wives in this way and the resultant disfigurements are appalling. I will never forget one lady I saw. From behind she appeared to be walking along the road (there are no pavements) on her knees. When we overtook her, I saw that from the knee downward her legs were stretched out in front of her and she was pushing them on ahead of her. There are men and even children in the roads, amongst the traffic propelling themselves along at ground level on homemade trolleys because they cannot walk. One of my local colleagues in the office is married to a top plastic surgeon here. They get a lot of practice.

This sounds pretty negative. There are some quaint and memorable sights. Not many animals around – but all through the three weeks that I have been here so far, on the route we take into the office every morning, on a busy main road, there are some railings where the road is effectively a bridge over a stretch of lake, and tied to that bridge every day are three, sometimes four cattle – the Asian variety with the big humps on the shoulders and beautiful colouring. They have baskets of feed and the road around them is kept clean – but it seems so odd to see them there day after day. They wouldn't know themselves if someone put them into a large green field!

One day, driving through some side roads in Banani – a mainly residential area and comparatively quiet – there tied to a small tree was a full-size buffalo! There are bananas everywhere and the little roadside stalls that spring up are selling them. Men are to be seen everywhere carrying huge baskets of them on their heads. It's amazing too to see what can be transported on the numerous pedal powered little carts. Mountains of chairs stacked up one on another, huge bales of cloth and even a cow strapped down on its side! The mind boggles to think how they got it there! There are bananas everywhere! Carried in baskets on heads, growing everywhere, piled on street seller's stalls. There are 600,000 rickshaws in Dhaka and drivers hire them for 200 taka for 8 hours during which they hope to make 500 takas – 300 profit (£3.50). There are garment sweatshops where 10-year-old girls labour 10 hour days and 7 day weeks for 10 taka a day.

I find it more relaxed in some ways than Pakistan and yet it is very violent. I saw stats today which indicated that in the last eight weeks there have been 600 murders; 550 road accidents; 120 rapes and 25 kidnappings.

It was a privilege at the weekend to visit the home of Patrick and his family. Patrick is our office driver and has taken me everywhere I needed to go and on Saturday he took me to his village about half an hour's drive out of the city. Patrick and his family are Christians. His very elderly father fought for the British in the second world war. Their houses were small and basic. There was no running water and no electricity. Patrick's wife did the washing up in the courtyard where there was a water pump. She didn't speak any English. The village was quiet and seemed peaceful, with areas of beautiful jasmine and hibiscus rich in colour and perfume. However, the majority of the village were Muslims and times can be tough for Patrick and the few other Christians in the village, particularly around Christmas apparently. Patrick's lovely daughter Ruth who is ten, sang a hymn to me in both Bangla and English. She wants to be a doctor when she grows up! I must send her some books when I get home.

It was weird on Sunday going to church in bare feet – and what a contrast to visit the beautiful International School set apart in Besundhara. As I ponder my first weeks here, I recognise the usual confusion of my heart and mind! How will we ever "overcome" terrorism when this huge level of disadvantage exists? What is being a western Christian about in this country? Is there an answer? Could I stay here long term? Are we actually helping??

I made trips to Singapore to run some training for our office staff there, and I did a brief trip to Azerbaijan based around training as well. That was my only trip to a former USSR country – and it takes a bit of getting used to that there are vodka shot glasses on the table with every meal including breakfast! Speaking of which, one of my most memorable meals was in Baku. The restaurant was actually an old caravanserai. Baku was on the original silk trail from China to Europe and our restaurant would have been a stopover with individual stalls for the camels built around a central courtyard. Each stall had been fitted out with a low level table and easy couch type seating with handmade blankets and cushions littered around, and the courtyard was lit by blazing medieval torches fixed on high poles around the yard. The food served to our party in our snug stall was buffet style; lots of individual dishes that were very Turkish / Persian with lots of fragrant fresh herbs and tender lamb, (and a pause for toasts in vodka every few minutes!) Memorable!!

But my most memorable trip was also my last one. It was the most scary, truly scary. Life threatening in fact. But it was an enormous privilege.

Afterthought: "What you do makes a difference, and you have to decide what kind of difference you want to make"
Jane Goodall

Chapter 11: Career Girl (2)

"Commit to the Lord whatever you do, and He will establish your plans" Proverbs 16:3

On September 11th, 2001, I watched in horror with colleagues on a TV set in the office as the twin towers came down in New York.

The following month, President George Bush demanded that the Taliban regime in Afghanistan extradite Osama Bin Laden the then leader of al Qaeda which they refused to do. American forces then began an invasion of Afghanistan with the intention of toppling the Taliban regime and denying militants a safe base of operation there, and they had liberated the capital Kabul by December of that year. Subsequently, the International Conference on Reconstruction Assistance to Afghanistan was held at ministerial in Tokyo in January and sixteen billion dollars was pledged by major donors including Britain.

Crown Agents was one of the first organisations to follow the Americans into Kabul with emergency supplies and subsequently with an international team of procurement consultants to begin utilising some of that donor funding to get Afghanistan up and running. I was privileged to be the UK based project manager for that part of the reconstruction effort. Kabul had once been a vibrant, romantic city on the silk route and in modern times a centre for the Hippie Trail with quality universities and known as the Paris of the East. Years of war had changed that. Afghanistan was not a functioning country. As our team started to arrive in Kabul, there was no office equipment, no computers, no landline telephone service, no postal service, no railways and no civil service - they had not been paid for five years, so were not sitting around in their offices.

Crown Agents had won a contract from the British Department for International Development to get government up and running together with a World Bank funded project worth 6.1 million dollars over 2 years. My colleagues and I had recruited a team of procurement experts from Britain, Bulgaria, Bangladesh, Nepal, Philippines, Romania, plus a Gambian, together with three Afghan members of the team. We rented a couple of houses in Kabul to house them – there were no functioning hotels - and I was managing the day-to-day relationships with the team members and with our clients. Several months into the project it was agreed that I should make a trip over there to meet them all face to face and to conduct some training. It was an exciting prospect but not a little scary.

There were no commercial airlines that flew into Kabul airport because it was not well enough equipped to either land or service large commercial flights. I had to fly to Dubai, then transfer to Sharjah for a local flight onwards to Kabul. The office had tried to book me onto a military flight into Kabul as they were considered safest but that didn't work out for timing. I landed in Dubai around midnight and was booked into an airport hotel for a few hours before being due at Sharjah at 5.00 am. I asked the hotel to book me a taxi for just after 4.00 am and tried to get some sleep. The taxi arrived on time, and I assumed had been told by the hotel where I needed to go. Apparently not. The driver spoke virtually no English, and I did my best to convey that we were going to Sharjah and the airport. We left the hotel, and I became somewhat concerned as at every junction or traffic light my driver was winding down his window, attracting the attention of other drivers and I realised he was asking for directions! This was worrying and I was working hard at staying in a place of peace! I didn't then realise quite how much this trip was going to test my prayer capacity! We were very soon out in open desert and the road ahead was straight and dark and I could only pray that it was the right road.

Oh, me of little faith! We duly arrived at Sharjah and the airport, and I booked in and arrived in the boarding lounge. I was of course suitably dressed. I had long trousers, long sleeves and my head was covered in a long black, beaded scarf. The boarding lounge filled up with a mixture of Arab and Afghan men. There were two other women, both with men who were obviously husbands and both very well covered. It was time to board. A steward arrived and opened the door onto the tarmac, and we began to file out. Then he stopped the procession and came to me and indicated that I was to board the plane first on my own! So, I was singled out of the crowd and ushered towards the open door at the rear of the plane. There was no seat numbers allocated, so I was invited to choose where I would like to sit. It was a medium sized plane, probably twenty rows of six across, so I chose a window seat around the middle of the plane. It began to fill up, but it became clear that none of the men felt comfortable coming to sit beside me! Seats were running out when a charming young Afghan guy appeared at the seat and kindly said that he would come and sit next to me and pretend that I was his mother!!

The plane was clearly quite old and well used. The seats were tired, and the seat belts the same. For the major part of the flight we were flying over the Hindu Kush mountain range; mile after mile of dense, impenetrable rocky peaks. I found myself thinking "If this plane goes down they would never get to us and my children will never know where my body is"! Cheerful thoughts. Not for the last time on this trip I had to rebuke myself and practise taking every thought captive to Christ once more.

The descent into Kabul is spectacular as the city sits high in a valley of the Hindu Kush at almost 6,000 feet above sea level. The descent has to be quite short and steep. At that time the one runway was uneven, so the landing was bumpy and as we taxied towards the small low level terminal building, there was evidence of war everywhere. The whole airport was littered with the wreckage of military Russian aircraft, vehicles and tanks. As we disembarked it became obvious that there was to be no standing on ceremony in entering the country. I had my passport and documents ready and was expecting the usual queue through immigration but instead there was a literal stampede of men towards the building which left me trailing well behind. Consequently, I was last through passport control and found myself facing baggage reclaim ……. It transpired that there was one carousel, but it was broken, and suitcases were just being thrown out into a heap and all the male passengers were scrambling to grab them. I was on the edge of panic as I saw my case being manhandled here and there in the chaos but there was no way I could get through all these men! Just then, someone touched my shoulder, and I turned to see a big guy in Afghan dress holding a Crown Agents identification and saying my name. It turned out to be Shabir, or Shabs for short, who turned out to be my rock in time of need! He muscled through the melee of men and grabbed my case and escorted me through customs (quite how he'd got through to airside himself, I never found out!)

I was staying in one of the houses the office had rented, along with a couple of other guys working for CA on the project. It was a large, spacious house in what was obviously an upmarket residential area. It was not plush, but it was comfortable and had a lovely garden which fascinated me as it could have been an English garden. It was June and there were roses, and lupins and daisies – quite bizarre. Kabul has the reputation as the sunniest capital city in the world, although the summer temperatures rarely go over 30 degrees centigrade and whilst I was there it was a very bearable 26 degrees on average. At least, it would have been bearable had I not had to be covered head to foot all the time!

It was lovely to meet all the guys in the team. Some I had met in London; some I had only spoken to by phone and the Afghans of course I had not met at all. I was most impressed with the Afghan people that I met. The guys working on our team were mostly quite young, had had mixed experience of education under the Taliban regime but were so eager to learn. I did some personality profiling work with the whole team as part of the work I was doing to strengthen team dynamics. Several of the international team had not come across the process before but the Afghans were particularly fascinated to start focussing on and recognising their individual character traits. I found I had a team of introverts on my hands – not at all unusual amongst procurement people, who need to be strong on detail, and therefore my task was to major in encouraging them to work harder at their communication, which is key to effective team performance!

Up until that point in my life, I had never been particularly concerned about the specific rights of women. The 1960's "burn your bra" campaign had largely passed me by, and on becoming a Christian, I rather adopted the then prevalent view in the church that "women should obey their husbands". I have since revised that view somewhat, but more of that in a coming chapter! However, I met some wonderful Afghan women whilst I was there. Women who held university degrees in medicine, engineering, languages, who were in their thirties and just re-emerging from the five-year house imprisonment imposed on them by the Taliban. They had been forced from their careers and not allowed out of their homes unless accompanied by a husband, father or brother. They had "used" those years to have their children and now were desperate to find their place in society once more. They were grieving over the generation of girls who had missed out on education under the Taliban, and I also heard horrific stories of women who had been imprisoned for offences of wearing makeup or being inappropriately dressed. And worse still the desperate young girls sold into marriage by their fathers to much older widowed men. These girls were often therefore pregnant at a very young age with resulting medical complications. But, and this is unbelievable, the older traditional men will not allow the intervention of doctors because their wives' bodies must not be seen. And of course, the qualified women doctors were locked up at home not allowed out! So, it was up to village midwives and women generally, to minister to each other. Consequently, the death in childbirth rate was the highest in the world at that time: 165 deaths in every 1,000 deliveries.

And it got worse. I began to receive an internet download of any and every news story about Afghanistan day by day, and I began to read about the suicide attempts of young women in the remote village areas. With limits to what is available the main methods are hanging, rat poison and setting fire to themselves. One rare set of figures from Herat, the third largest city, showed that out of 123 suicides, 106 were women. I was several times driven past the main stadium in Kabul where public executions were regularly carried out under the old regime. A young woman decapitated under accusation of adultery. I thought of Jesus and the story the young woman caught out in adultery in John 7. How different my faith and my God is to the cruel control exerted as a result of an extreme Muslim faith.

I began to be really stirred about these women. Such injustice. But now, with the allies in charge and holding security, things will start to improve.

Back at the house, we had a male Afghan cook, who rarely came out of the kitchen, a driver whom I saw frequently, and Rosaria the cleaner, a lovely Afghan woman probably in her late thirties or early forties. We were the only women in the house but couldn't converse. She only spoke Pashtun and my English, French and German were all useless! We exchanged smiles and some miming. She made it clear she wanted to paint my hands with henna, a practise called Mehndi. I wasn't too keen and so a couple of times managed to indicate "maybe tomorrow". But when tomorrow came, Rosario didn't turn up for work as usual. And neither did she on the second day. We asked the driver to go past her house and see if she was ok. What he came back and told us was shocking. Apparently, one of our guys had taken a couple of photos in the garden one day of a couple of them posing with Rosaria and had given her copies. There was absolutely nothing compromising about the photos; just three people standing together in a garden. But apparently Rosaria's husband found the photos and had beaten her so severely that she had been unable to get off her bed for two days. He had beaten her so severely in fact that he had damaged his own hand. He had sought medical help for his hand but there was no such help for his wife. And there would be no retribution for him; no police involvement; no assault charges. He was within his rights to discipline his wife. I didn't see Rosaria again before I left Kabul. The guys in the house felt so guilty for their unwitting part in her pain. It was a lesson learned and a memory I will not forget.

I was enjoying my trip. The office stuff was going well, I loved the people and the work, but there were constant reminders everywhere that this was not a peaceful place. Everywhere I went, there were the remains of bombed out buildings, children begging, women in the blue bourka that belonged to Kabul (other cities in Afghanistan wore white bourkas) were a constant reminder of the fragile freedom they had. There was frequently the sound of n mortar fire somewhere in the distance. And one evening, as we were enjoying a BBQ in our garden (the guys in the house had conjured up the most ingenious BBQ made mostly of old oil drums) there was a loud noise and we all rushed into the house as a couple of rockets went overhead. So, it was tense, and I was aware of having to control my fear – which meant praying quietly a lot of the time – practising the presence of the God I trusted to keep me safe.

One of my colleagues in Kabul was also a Christian. We had known one another back in London as we both were part of the Crown Agents' Christian Union. I had joined it when I started there and had somehow ended up leading it. We were usually about a dozen and met weekly at lunchtime and did some bible study and prayer together, and every year we organised a Crown Agents' Carol Service at the parish church opposite our building with an invitation to all staff. It was always well attended with a hundred and more members of staff turning up.

Anyway, Andy asked me if I'd like to go to church on Friday. The working week had Fridays and Saturdays off, but we worked on Sundays. He explained that it would depend on whether he could find out where it was going to be held as the venue changed week by week for security reasons. He also said that it was usually ok, but they did have always an armed guard outside the door. We were in an extremist Muslim country which had no tolerance for other faiths. He arranged to pick me up at nine o'clock the next morning.

I was ready when Andy arrived and was sorry to hear that he had made several phone calls but couldn't find out where church would be held, so thought he would take me sightseeing instead. He suggested we head out to the DuralAman Palace, southwest of the city centre. It had apparently been constructed in the 1920's by the then Emir but had been badly damaged in the civil wars. We drove out through parts of the city I had not seen before, always with the imposing backdrop of the Hindu Kush mountains in the background. The palace was situated on the top of a hill and as we approached, I could see a driveway winding up the hill towards a large imposing building. However, we were stopped at the bottom of the drive by an armed military person and after a conversation between him and our driver, it transpired that the palace was off limits, something to do with insurgents and a bomb.

So, change of plan, we headed back into the city to have a coffee at the only functioning hotel in town, the Intercontinental. We got through the security check and got settled in the lounge with our coffee, when there was a commotion in the lobby and a load of armed soldiers came rushing through to evacuate the hotel. There was a threat of a bomb.

That afternoon, I was scheduled to attend the UN security briefing at Bagram, the American army base. I sat through the briefing which was reporting on the security status of every region of the country. The last area to be reported was Kabul. I then listened as the senior military officer announcing that at the DuralAman Palace the previous evening two insurgents had been setting a trip wire bomb across the main front door, when it had exploded on them, and they had both been killed.

I went cold. And felt sick. A trip wire across the main door. Andy and I were there just after nine this morning. It was not a place many people went to. There is every probability that Alex and I would have been the first to go through that door. As all this was dawning in my mind, I sort of heard another voice in my mind repeating some words that I recognised as scripture. They went over and over. I thought they were maybe from the book of Isaiah. I felt weak with shock as my mind was thinking what if,,,,, what if,

When I got back to the house, I searched through my bible. Yes, I found the verse that had been running through my mind.

"For I am the Lord your God, the Holy one of Israel, your Saviour; I give Egypt for your ransom, Cush and Sheba in your stead. Since you are precious and honoured in my sight, and because I love you, I will give people in exchange for you, nations in exchange for your life" Isaiah 43:3-4

Oh goodness! I suddenly felt the fear, the fear of vulnerability, the vulnerability of chance. I could have been killed. That would have been international news. My poor family.

But I wasn't. I was spared. But two people lost their lives. Two men who were also sons, husbands, fathers, brothers, self-destructed. What a waste. How stupid this all is. Terrorism, violence, hatred, fear.

But I was spared. Thank you, Father. Thank you. But why? Why me? So many people have died needlessly in this conflict. Why me?

And then I'm on my knees, sobbing and thanking God. Saying thank you Lord, over and over. Praying for the families of the two dead men. Praying for the stupid hostilities to stop.

Suddenly I wanted to go home. To be safe.

The flight out of Kabul went straight to Dubai where I had an overnight in an airport hotel. I booked in to my room and immediately ran a bath! (There had been a very unreliable, meagre shower in Kabul). I lay in that bath for ages, soaking the stress out of my body, and praising the Saviour who truly had given his life to save me. Then I had a room service meal and watched a silly film on the TV.

And that was Afghanistan. A beautiful, tragic country, which after a mere twenty years of something like democracy, is currently back to square one. I pray for those people. Especially the women.

Afterthought: "Optimism for me isn't a passive expectation that things will get better; it's a conviction that we can make things better – that whatever suffering we see, no matter how bad it is, we can help people if we don't lose hope, and we don't look away" Melinda Gates

Chapter 12: Moving on

"...the snare has been broken, and we have escaped! Psalm 124: 7(b)

By the early 1990's I was well established in my career, both my son and my daughter were married, as were Susie and the various other young women I have written about. I was still living in the house owned by the fellowship Trust but now on my own with two ageing dogs. For some time at church I had been feeling uneasy. I had committed myself to the church prayer meetings which I thoroughly enjoyed, and I felt I had grown some in my understanding of prayer. The original pastor's wife had also moved on, and I had inherited responsibility for the women's meetings. I had managed to make some good contacts, and we had some well-known female speakers visiting whom I was privileged to host and introduce. Some of them were prophetic and there were times when they spoke some powerful prophetic words over me personally.

I had also followed my heart for the young mums in the church. Most of them had husbands who were involved in the leadership of the church as well as doing full time jobs, so these mums were therefore frequently at home with their children and missing out on church activities and fellowship. I so remembered being in that stage of life myself and feeling guilty because I felt I wasn't growing. So, bearing in mind the story in Luke chapter 10 about the two sisters Mary and Martha, I started up an evening group called "Martha and Me" just for young mums. We did some learning together along with praying for each other and chatting! We had some good times, and I remember one young mum actually went into labour on my sofa!!

I had tried to define the restlessness I felt. I had tried to push it aside. This time my restlessness was not with myself but with my church. I felt that the way the fall of the original minister four years or so back now, was dealt with was not as thoroughly as it should have been and that the church was struggling as a result. I felt as though I kept bumping my head on some sort of invisible ceiling – because I was a woman. And yet, I also held the view that my commitment to my church was like a marriage commitment – for better for worse; for richer for poorer. And I was not the one to break marriage commitments. But I was struggling to find fulfilment in this "marriage". I prayed about it endlessly, usually with the sense that it must be my fault that I wasn't more settled. Because my conviction that God is real, Jesus His son died for each one of us, and that through that death and resurrection he heralded in the opportunity for each of us to be restored in not only relationship with the God of the universe, but restored to His image as seen in Jesus as well, I looked around me and wondered why the church wasn't being more effective, not necessarily in what it did, but in seeing lives transformed.

At this time, I had become close to a couple in church who were actively involved in deliverance ministry. I had long ago repented of my early venture into the occult with the spiritualist Faith Healer but there were things I didn't feel happy about in my life, so I was willing to be prayed for. One of those things was that since the age of five, I had massacred my fingernails. I didn't actually bite them, but I picked them and tore at them in an act of self-harm until they bled and were sore. Consequently, I was always ashamed of my hands and usually did my best to hide them. Perhaps it was demonic so off I went for prayer. But nothing changed. I was party to joining this couple in praying for people who presented with issues that bothered them and we prayed demons out of all of them. However, when people submit themselves to prayer for deliverance, and then find their issue remains unresolved, there is a tendency for self- condemnation to creep in. I watched it in other people and knew it about myself. How hopeless am I if I get delivered of demons and yet still, I don't manage to leave my fingernails alone? There's something missing here! But I gritted my teeth, sought to stay loyal and kept going. But not very successfully. Often, I came out of church on a Sunday feeling worse than before I went in! Worse mainly about myself because I wasn't doing better! It was hard work.

One Monday morning in early 1994, I arrived in the office and was greeted excitedly by a young man on my team. Andrew was a Christian and was seeking God's purpose for his life as he felt called to ministry. He proceeded to share that at his church the previous night, a local Anglican church, they had played a voice recording by a well-known church leader who from had just returned from Canada where it seemed there was some sort of spiritual revival going on. Apparently just listening to this speaker describing their experience caused a stirring of the Holy Spirit for people with all sorts of reactions.

Over the next few weeks, The Toronto Blessing became news across the country. It had originated in The Airport Vineyard Fellowship in Toronto and was described as an outpouring of the Holy Spirit bringing an increased awareness of God's love and spontaneous worship accompanied by phenomena such as falling over under the power of the Spirit, spontaneous laughter, weeping and a sense of deep connection to God. I was curious – and so hungry for more of God – and my dear friend and prayer partner Margie and I very prayerfully started going to some of these meetings locally. We prayed for discernment, prayed against deception, and over and over again found ourselves being touched, encouraged and refreshed at the meetings we went to. By late summer, we were convinced and decided to go to Toronto ourselves! We booked a hotel near the church for a week, and then booked a lakeside cabin upcountry for a second week. On arrival at the hotel, everyone knew about the revival at the local church! All the taxi drivers knew about it! The church was an unpretentious converted shop on a small parade of local shops. There were constant queues outside it. The meetings were amazing!! The worship was a revelation! The songs, the musicians, the congregational response was a game changer! I was later to learn that the Vineyard Movement, of which this church was part, were renowned for worship and worship songs, and in fact many years later are generally credited with having changed the face of worship in many evangelical streams of church. The meetings were filled with people sharing accounts of how, why they were there and what God had been showing them. So many stories of lives impacted. We loved it. After our week, we transferred up country to a wonderful cedar cabin on a lakeside with a wonderful facility on site where we had time to relax and review all that we had experienced, but after four days, by mutual agreement, we cut short our stay, packed our bags and headed back to Toronto for another couple of days before our flight home.

On one of the several occasions that I found myself lying on the floor in that place, relaxed and fully conscious but overwhelmed by the sense of God's love and presence, I had a vivid picture. It was so clear that I was able to draw it afterwards and I have consequently never forgotten it. There was a very large fountain, built in white stone and rather like the one in Trafalgar Square, London, but higher. There were loads of people around it and Jesus, in traditional white robe, was perched on the bottom rim of the fountain and I was standing right next to him. Jesus was continually dipping cups into the water around the fountain and handing them out. He handed me a cup full of water, and I drank it, He handed me another, then another, then another. He kept on handing me cups of water and I kept drinking them dry. Then after a while, he handed me the cup….. and instead of drinking it, I passed it on., over and over again, passing numerous cups of water on to the crowd around us.

I saw all of this happening in my mind's eye so clearly, but I only superficially understood what it meant.

We flew home and the following Sunday, I optimistically set off for church. Surely, I would cope better now!

I didn't. I was uneasy, uncomfortable and wretched. That evening, I took the decision not to go to the evening service as I would always normally have done. I stayed home and decided to play one of the CDs I had bought in Toronto but had not yet listened to. It was called "My Father's House" by Brian Doerksen. I can remember in my wretchedness I was lying on the carpet in my living room beside the CD player as I listened. Second track in was a song called "There must be a place" . As I listened, I started to sob. "There must be a place"……. And then the lyrics went on "where I can fly free ". I sobbed and sobbed. And then, as clear as a bell, I heard a voice speaking to me, the voice of the Lord, and he said, "So what's the cage Wendy?". And I remembered the Bishop from Nigeria, five or six years before, sharing his dream of the bird in the cage. And I had got it wrong. Suddenly I knew,

"What's the cage Wendy?".

"Lord, it's the church".

"Yes, and the door is open, and you must fly free".

"But Lord, where should I go?"

"Where have you been most blessed?"

"Toronto?"

"No! The Vineyard Movement"

Oh, my goodness! I was shaking and sobbing and snotty, but it was now crystal clear. God had spoken to me, and I was going to obey. It would not be easy. Vineyard was in its infancy in Britain.

And there was at that time, only one church in my area about 35 minutes' drive away, where I knew nobody. But I would go.

Afterthought: The media thinks the church is dying. It isn't!

Chapter 13: Feeding in the field

"He has filled the hungry with good things…" Luke 1:53

The next Sunday morning I went on my own to the Vineyard Church nearest to me as the Lord had indicated. It met in a large secondary school and the car park was already looking very busy when I arrived. I was greeted by friendly people and was ushered towards coffee and, wonder of wonders, fresh doughnuts!! Amazing! I found my way into the main hall which was already buzzing with people and found a seat. The service started with worship and the first song we sang was one I had learned in Toronto! The second was another we had sung there, and which still always stirs me to tears. The song is called "Isn't He beautiful" and is a simple love song about Jesus. As we were singing that song, I had a picture, as clear as the one I'd had in Toronto, but this time I was sat cross legged on some grass in a field. I was in a whole circle of people sitting on the grass and on my left-hand side sat Jesus. We were having a picnic together! Jesus had a hunk of bread in his hand, and as I watched he threw his head back laughing heartily about something and I could see he had been chewing on the bread! I wanted to remind him that you shouldn't eat with your mouth open but didn't! It was all very relaxed and easy going, then Jesus stood up and started heading out across the field, indicating that I should follow him, so I saw myself scramble to my feet and begin to follow.

The worship ended and the Senior Pastor got up to preach and announced that he was continuing his series that morning on "The role of women in church"! I sat and listened, and the tears began to gently slide down my face. This is where I should be! I had come home! At the end of the meeting people flocked to the front for prayer (I was used to having to form an orderly queue in front of the Pastor) and I found myself joining them. A lovely lady appeared and prayed for me. I can't remember anything about what she prayed but I left feeling as though I had met with God. I was loved, accepted, validated and excited!

Later that same day I went back for the evening service. The same Senior Pastor spoke, but this time he spoke about church planting. In all my years as a Christian so far, I had never even thought about church planting, let alone hear anyone preach about it. But I was really struck about that. Why had I never thought about it before! Of course, it made sense! How amazing! People could, and should, be ready to respond to a call to plant churches! But I had zero expectation of ever actually being involved.

I did my best to leave my original church well, seeking their blessing. It was sad. I had been there for thirteen years. My children had grown up there; all my friendships were there but Jesus had asked me to follow him onwards and I was going to obey.

Southwest London Vineyard (SWLV) was a big church, and it took a while to find my feet. I joined a small group which I loved and got involved in feeding the homeless on the South Bank in London which the church did every Sunday lunchtime, taking up hot meals which a team had prepared and cooked in the school kitchens whilst the morning meeting was going on. A very few weeks in, I went to a mid-week training evening on deliverance. I felt I'd been there and got the t-shirt, but was interested to see how it would be handled. That evening proved to be another significant turning point for me. The person teaching explained that human beings are fallen and broken people and consequently have lots of damage, resulting in fears, habits, anxieties etc which manifest in our daily lives as dysfunctions of various sorts. In fact, they suggested, 90% of human dysfunction come from woundedness of heart and mind and the other 10% of issues might be demonic. However, they went on to say, if we bring

Jesus into that wounding and bring truth and healing into it, then the enemy has much less to hang on to and leaves. Now then, I had been previously taught the opposite. That 90% of human dysfunction is demonic and needs deliverance. Hmm. I need to think about this.

I was reminded that a year or so previously, I had given in to a friend's constant nagging and gone to a conference led by Lianne Payne who wrote and taught healing through union with Christ . One thing had stuck vividly in my mind. She had taught one session about the need for healing of memories that cause us pain; and when in conclusion she had invited people to stand for prayer, the attractive young woman sat in front of me had suddenly fallen to the floor, writhing and screaming. Ah, I thought to myself as ministry team members came to her and helped her into a side room for prayer, thats a need for deliverance if ever I saw one. Later that evening, Leanne was inviting people onto the platform to share testimony, and this same young lady responded. Imagine how chastened and ashamed I was as she recounted that as Leanne had prayed in the morning session, she had remembered the pain and fear and panic that she had experienced when she was severely sexually abused as a five-year old child. She had not been writhing under the influence of Satan but had been reliving the surfaced memory of that awful experience – and experiencing it exactly as the child did. As she stood on the platform explaining her story she was radiant with peace and healing.

I went on to do some training at SWLV and then ministered in inner healing for many years to many people in my church, and it is proven to me without a shadow of a doubt that human beings are broken and wounded by the broken world in which we live and that the need for deliverance is usually secondary to the need for receiving the healing love of Jesus through prayer.

I was also enjoying a new sense of freedom in worship and the concept of "practising " the presence of God with me at all times and in all places. I began to practise communicating with the Father and the Son as I went about my day, constantly aware that He is my constant companion, teacher and friend. I was loving being part of a small group of people who met together in the week to worship together and learn together and pray for each other. I found there a level of trust and vulnerability that was life giving and which I had never experienced before. This was a bunch of people for whom following Jesus was personal, humbling and healing.

The Vineyard Movement was started by a guy called John Wimber in California in the early 1980s. It is classed as a "neo-charismatic evangelical protestant "church movement. In reality, its formed around followers of Jesus who major around worship as well as praise, singing songs to the Lord as well as praise songs about Him. They also aim to actually "do the stuff" that Jesus did, i.e. healing the sick, delivering people from the demonic and extend a genuine welcome to "come as you are". It was also very clear that although you are welcome to "come just as you are", you are expected not to "stay as you are" because walking with Jesus means transformational change. All these ideas were new to me and so refreshing. It was also clear that women were free to be who they are, using their gifts and talents in the Lord's service in an atmosphere of mutual respect and non-threat. And indeed, both men and women were free to lead, share in ministry to the body, i.e the body ministering to the body, and be loved, accepted and respected for who God had created then to be. All of this to me was like trying on a new wardrobe of clothes, taking off the outdated ones and trying new ones on for size! I found these new garments fitted me well and were very comfortable to wear! And as I read the scriptures through my new spectacles, I found that wearing my new clothes fitted me into God's story and gave me room to grow.

And so a couple of years passed by and I began to feel completely at home in this new church; new friends, deeper understanding, growing confidence and joy, so much joy.

NB I also noticed that after a while in this atmosphere of body ministry. i.e. being prayed for and praying for others I stopped taking out anxiety and tension on my fingernails and my growing inner peace was reflected in the fact that my fingernails grew!!

And then it was all change again!

Afterthought: Albert Einstein made the claim that "if you feed your mind as often as you feed your stomach, you'll never have to worry about feeding your stomach or roof over your head or clothes on your back". That may well be true, but I rather suspect that it's what we consume that's critical! It's surely crucial to feed our minds on things of substance and truth rather than trivia and trash, just as its best to fill our stomachs with nourishing wholefoods rather than fast food and goodies!

Chapter 14: Homelessness on the Horizon

"Foxes have dens and birds in the sky have nests, but the Son of Man has no place to lay his head" Luke 9:58

I loved the weekly Small Group that I had joined at SWLV. We met together in the home of the leaders and week by week we worshipped together, learned from the Bible and prayed for each other. I was just getting to feel comfortable and confident in that environment, when some difficult news hit. The Trust that owned my house wanted to sell it! The trustees had decided to sell all assets and dissolve the Trust. Oh! Help! What now!

I had been privileged to live in this house, which I loved, for 17 years. It had been my haven and my security through so much. It had been a temporary home to so many and the home which my children would most remember. It had seen us through times of pain and heartache, but it had seen times of healing and growth as well.

I had never paid rent, but I had paid all the bills. Bearing in mind this was a four bedroomed detached house of generous proportions, those bills were never small, and during those years I had also been financially responsible for two children, on firstly no income but Family Allowance, then on basic maintenance from the divorce, and then on income from a part time job in which I had started pretty near the bottom of the pay scale! In other words, I did not have money in the bank awaiting just such an eventuality as this!

So, along with the lovely people in my Small Group, I began to pray. Things moved fast. The house went on the market and sold very quickly. One of the advantages of the sale was that there was no chain because I was obligated to move out straight away! By this time, my prayers were getting desperate. I was looking at the property pages of the local paper and feeling utterly overwhelmed with the amounts of money required.

One evening, when the house was under offer but not finalised, and I was no nearer a solution to the problem, I went to dinner with my friend and prayer partner, Margie. She had also invited Paul & Chris. Chris I knew well as she had been part of the damaging fellowship , but Paul was the new man in her life, a very new Christian (who had come to faith through an encounter with an angel) and neither Margie nor I had met him before. The evening progressed well – dinner at Margie's was always a lovely experience – and we were still sitting at the dinner table over coffee, when it became obvious in the middle of our chat that Paul was looking a bit uncomfortable. It transpired that he was experiencing a strange tingling in his right arm along with an increasing heat. Inexperienced though he was, he was confident it was from God and thought it was something to do with me. At the same time, I found some words echoing though my head that I thought might be from the book of Isaiah. Margie produced a Bible, and I eventually found the words. They were from Isaiah Chapter 41 v 13 *"For I am the Lord your God who takes hold of your right hand and says to you "Do not fear; I will help you"*. Wow!

I suggested to Paul that maybe he needed to take my right hand in his as a sort of prophetic action. Paul stretched across the table. I thought he would take my right hand in his as in a handshake, but he didn't. Instinctively with his downturned right hand he clasped my right forearm so that my upturned right hand grasped the underside of his forearm. I have pondered that and researched it since. An ordinary handshake is an open gesture that indicates equality. The way Paul reached for my arm indicated the superior downward grasp of authority, whilst my instinctive response was upward to receive the clasp in an attitude of surrender. Interesting! And in that moment of hand clasp, I had a picture fleetingly but out of nowhere of a key being passed to me; an old fashioned, large, wrought iron type of door key. A key to my future home? Or a metaphorical key to my future?

Anyway, as soon as we had done this, the physical sensations left Paul completely and we continued our evening together whilst I pondered this interesting intervention. It felt as though God was underlining that He knew my predicament and was committed to me in it in some way. Could that be true? It was a very tentative feeling. I knew that God was real and had heard many amazing and validated accounts of just how He can and does intervene in the lives of people, but my confidence that I could be one of those people was pretty low. I decided to tell the others that I had seen a picture, but not tell them it was a picture of a key and asked that they would pray that God would confirm the picture to me somehow.

The next morning, I did something I have not done before or since! I woke myself up talking!! I was saying audibly over and over again "The 23rd of October, the 23rd of October, the 23rd of October". Strange. I mentally checked the date. The date I was waking up to was Sunday 20th October! That coming Wednesday 23rd I was due to go to hear a prophetic speaker and Bible teacher from America at the home of the local leader of the Lydia Prayer Fellowship, a lady called Dr Tamara (Tammy) Winslow. Strange.

Wednesday 23rd October arrived, and I went to the local meeting with my friend Margie as arranged. There were about 20 people crammed into the living room of the house and Tammy opened the meeting leading worship, seated at the grand piano in the room. I had never met her before, nor did I speak to her before the meeting began. We were all singing in worship, when she suddenly stopped mid verse and spoke out "The Lord wants you to know that the picture you saw is right!" I felt as though someone had punched me in the chest. I gasped. I felt that God was speaking to me! But no, hang on. Things like that don't happen to me! "No Lord, I need more than that; she could mean anyone". She resumed playing and singing and everyone joined in. A couple of minutes later, she stopped mid-song again and spoke out "The Lord is giving you the key tonight!" Oh my. Was this my confirmation? Surely it had to be! Tammy went on to teach powerfully from the story of Joseph in Genesis and about the significance of outer garments in his life with the message that the Lord's plan is to clothe us in new garments but first we have to let the old garments go. It was powerful teaching and my heart and spirit responded powerfully.

The house sale concluded just after Christmas and with nothing else on the horizon, I arranged for all my goods and furniture to be stored in friends' garages and myself and the two dogs temporarily moved in with my retired brother and sister-in-law who lived locally and who had a spare bedroom. I hated having to be dependent. My brother was proactive in trying to help me move on. Often, I would get back from work and find he had been to local Estate Agents and picked up details of local flats for sale for me. I felt under pressure. I had an appointment with a local building society and ascertained to my surprise that I could potentially get a mortgage despite the fact that I was now in my early 50s. So I started to spend evenings and weekends viewing potential flats to buy. I still had the two dogs and so needed access to a garden if at all possible. Over a couple of months, I went to view well over a dozen potential flats as in ground floor two-bedroom flats. (I felt I needed two bedrooms at least as my daughter and her husband and my baby grandson lived 150 miles away and so needed to be able to stay over when they visited). Each time I took someone with me to the viewing, usually Margie and each time we would leave the property with her saying "You can't possibly live there"! We saw some dire properties! Either they were really bad conversions, or had damp, or were in impossible locations, and although I was desperate and could probably have raised the finance, none of them felt right. None of them felt like God was involved despite the fact that I was continually crying out to Him for help and felt I had

had His affirmation that He was there for me. He had given me a key.

About this time, I remember being up in our local park walking my dogs. The park was a special place to me, one I visited regularly, often at the end of a tiring day in the office, and as the dogs ran and sniffed and had their freedom, I would pray. At one time, after the Great Storm of October 1987, in which this park amongst many others lost hundreds of trees, there was a particularly well-situated log left amidst the carnage, which gave a wonderful view and which became my prayer log, where I would sit as the dogs roamed about and I would pray. On this occasion however, I was walking the length of the park, once again bending God's ear about my need for somewhere to live. All of a sudden, I felt a stillness come over me, and I stopped walking. I felt a voice inside asking "What do you really want Wendy?" What do I want? I rehearsed in my head all the various attributes that would constitute a dream home: a cottage in a quiet road; roses round the door; three bedrooms to allow for guests, a garden for the dogs; all mod cons….. and then I landed. "Lord". I eventually replied, "I just want a home that nobody can take away from me again". Something I had not had for almost twenty years.

Eventually after four months at my brother's, I found myself for the third time in my life with an ultimatum to move on. First from Holly Hill, then from the Fellowship house, and now from my brother's. Would I ever again have a home nobody could make me leave? The next provision came via my lovely small group at church. As I shared the fact that I needed to move on but had had no success in finding somewhere to buy, I was offered the temporary use of a three-bedroom house in the immediate area. It belonged to one of the couple's elderly mothers who was just relocating to a care home at least on a temporary basis and maybe permanently. It was an eleventh-hour rescue opportunity, and I gratefully accepted it.

It turned out to be a nice house in a good locality, but it was of course full of the elderly lady's furniture and household goods, most of which were also rather elderly! Nevertheless, I moved in with relief. I paid a nominal rent and was responsible for household bills. At least I was no longer a guest and had my own space once again although to start with I felt disoriented and anxious as it was likely to be a very short-term arrangement.

About 3 months after moving into this house, and still feeling rather low, still disoriented and insecure, something really strange happened. Every night as I get ready for bed, I sit at the dressing table, clean my face and systematically remove my jewellery i.e. my watch, earrings and rings. At the time I was wearing my mother's wedding ring and eternity ring and on this particular evening, I removed them as usual and placed them on the dressing table – as usual. (All my own jewellery had been stolen a couple of years before when the house was broken into on three separate occasions). The next morning, getting ready to go to work, I went to replace everything; my watch, earrings and…… where were the two rings? They weren't there! They must be! They weren't! I went back over the events of the previous evening. What had I done? My mind was blank. I didn't remember the usual process. But then, how often do we do things on automatic pilot and not specifically remember the process! My watch and earrings were there, so I had clearly taken those off in the usual way….. but no rings. I search the dressing table surface, moved everything, checked the drawers, checked underneath it and behind it…..no rings. It was time to go to work. The missing rings were on my mind all day. As soon as I got home, I pulled the bedroom apart; moved everything, stripped the bedding, as well as checking the bathroom and all the floor space. No rings.

Two days later, I had an unexpected contact from a friend asking if she and her husband could possibly drop by and stay the night the following day as she had a family emergency and need to overnight in the area. As my bedroom had the double bed, I cleaned the room, changed the bed and vacated the room for the guests. When they arrived and I showed them up, I explained that my rings had gone missing three days before and would they please keep an eye open for them. My guests left and I moved back into the main bedroom. Two days later, the alarm went off, I woke up, sat up in bed, and there on the dressing table were my two missing rings!!! I couldn't believe it. What was happening. "Lord, is this you? I don't understand. This is supernatural. Why? What? Help me, Lord!"

It was only later that morning at work, as I went to type my first email of the day and entered the date…….. it was 23rd of October!!! One year on….. 23rd of October again! And some light dawned. Rings - they are a symbol of covenant. The right hand of fellowship is a symbol of covenant in many ancient traditions included in scripture and in more modern times, the giving and receiving of rings is also a symbol of covenant. In the year that had just passed I had been moved on from my long-term home, via my brother's hospitality and was still lodging in someone else's home on a temporary basis. The year had been full of anxiety, insecurity and a sense of failure in not providing for myself. God in His infinite kindness was reminding me that He is not a man that He should lie but is a covenant keeping, utterly faithful God and loving Father and he had given me a key.

You can imagine maybe with what a sense of awe and reverence I replaced those rings on my right hand. They had been hidden in the palm of the hand of the most high God for six days. How awesome!

I'd had to take a difficult decision about precious Toby whilst at my brother's. He apparently had a couple of minor strokes which had left him largely incontinent. That's difficult to manage for a dog particularly whilst I was at work all day, so once again I found myself taking a beloved dog for a last trip to the vet. This time however, I was paying the bill and so was able to stay with him and hold him and talk to him as he breathed his last. Then I went straight round to my son's and sobbed on his shoulder before having a comforting cuddle with my brand-new baby granddaughter. The Lord gives….. and the Lord takes away.

Not long after establishing myself and Bruno in our new home, he started exhibiting the same symptoms. I had expected him to be completely lost after Toby died, but in fact he hadn't batted an eyelid!! But there was now no doubting that he too was now on a limited timescale. After a couple of trips to the vet and clear confirmation that he was not going to get better, I took the decision that it was not fair to have to leave him on his own for nine hours a day with deteriorating eyesight and the potential for another stroke at any time. So, once again…. we went to the vet for the last time one evening. But this time, it was the end of the line. I knew I couldn't take on a new puppy in someone else's house which was temporary anyway, and I didn't know for how long or where I would end up next. I love dogs and feel strongly that as an owner you need to be able to commit to them long term with all that might mean. My future at that time was insecure. I did not know what it would look like. I came home to an empty house for the first time in over twenty-five years. No waggy tailed greeting and canine presence in the absence of human family.

The next day at work we were hosting a VIP visitor, and I was one of those giving a presentation to him. I knew my colleagues would ask me how Bruno was. Before I left home, I rang the office and spoke to the person who answered: "I am coming in. I will be there in time for the presentation. Just please tell everybody not to talk to me until it's over. I don't want to talk"!!! I walked into our department, and everybody studiously ignored me. Our VIP arrived; we did the presentation. He left. I walked back into the department.

Someone came up and put their arms around me … and I lost it!! Dogs!! They capture our hearts! Arguably the very best of God's creation!!!

I stayed in the elderly lady's house for almost two years, learning to live on my own with no dogs for company! But eventually the house needed to be sold to pay for her care and once again I was on an ultimatum to move on.

My Heavenly Father had sought to prepare me for this! He had bent over backwards to assure me that He was with me, that He had given me a key for the future, and yet I remember at the time feeling a bit like a rabbit caught in headlights. I knew there was a crisis, a decision had to be made, but I felt powerless and sort of frozen. Lord help me!

It came to crunch point, and I had taken no decisions. I had been praying. But that wasn't enough. So, I decided I would have to rent. At least I had no dogs to worry about now. Eventually I took a day off work to take a tour of local rental agents to find a two-bedroom flat. The first one I went into had literally apparently just acquired details of one becoming free. They hadn't yet got a prospectus printed for it, but they did have the key. Would I like to view it? I arranged with a friend to meet the agent there that afternoon. And I prayed some more. "Lord please show me if this is right! I don't want to make a wrong decision".

The flat turned out to be on the fourth floor of a ten-storey block in a convenient location. We met the agent and took the lift to the fourth floor. I walked into the flat and looked at the view. Spectacular. Hmm. "Could I live here? Father, I am fed up with temporary addresses. Is this home? "

However, the flats had been built with beautiful wood block flooring in the main living area, but as I took in things around me, it appeared that the wood floor had had channels cut across it that apparently took the piping to the radiators when central heating was installed. And then, believe it or not, these channels had been concreted over and painted brown!! It looked hideous and ruined what had been a beautiful floor. When the agent asked me if I was interested, I found myself saying that I might be, but that I couldn't live with the floor like that! She suggested I could put rugs over it. I desisted, saying no, it's so badly damaged it needs carpeting! She looked slightly surprised at my temerity and said that she'd have to ask the owners, and that they lived in the Caribbean and were very slow to respond to emails. I was praying in my head when I said to her "Well, you ask the owners and then I'll tell you whether I want it or not!"

I left the property, dropped my friend home and by the time I got in there was a message on my answerphone from the agent saying that she had spoken to the owners, and they had instructed her to get a quote for carpeting! Later that evening I spoke to a friend on the phone whom I had asked to pray for me that day as I went flat hunting. She wanted to know how I got on but before I told her, she said that as she had prayed that day, she just kept getting the word "pink" and seeing the colour pink and she supposed that maybe the right flat would have something pink.

I had noted that unusually the lift in the block I had been in had carpet up the inside walls of it and that carpet was pink! And in the actual flat the bedroom carpets were……. You've guessed it! Pink. It seemed that God had heard my cries for help and one way, or another was providing the affirmation I needed that this was the next place to live. It would not have been my first choice, but it was way better than any of those flats I'd viewed with an option to buy. And I wasn't in a place to be too choosy.

Afterthought: The charity Crisis states that the reasons for homelessness include poverty, systematic inequality and discrimination, and incomes that fail to keep up with rising rents and the cost of living. All of these social issues put immense pressure on people. A stable home is a foundation we all need. Homelessness is far more than "rooflessness" or lack of physical shelter. It is the lack of a home. I used to be part of a volunteer ministry from church that took hot meals up to rough sleepers on the Embankment in London on Sunday lunchtimes, and the stories of the homeless people I met up there were unique and heartbreaking.

Chapter 15: The Slippery Slope.

"He makes my feet like the feet of a deer, he enables me to tread on the heights" Habakkuk 3:19

The Agent of the flat ordered the carpet for fitting in the lounge, I paid a small deposit and my references were accepted. It was all going ahead. There was one problem. I was going to need a considerable sum of money to cover the full deposit plus a month's rent in advance before I could move in, which I did not have.

I had been paying my way in full since I had moved out of the fellowship house, but against a background of being at the beginning of a salary scale again, and the lack of background of solid financial habits. I had never been taught about money management, never been encouraged to save and, indeed, had not had a lot of opportunity to build those habits for myself, given the fact that I'd only been earning regularly for a couple of years before I was married, and my husband then took control of joint finance. My father had always had a tendency to be over-cautious with money – he himself had grown up with a dad who liked to gambol and of course he had lived through the Great Depression of the 30s. My mum had never earned since she had been married and neither of them thought to lay a foundation for me in money management! I am generous by nature and frequently earned rebukes for that, but without the encouragement to plan and save!

But I was by then entirely responsible for my finances and needed to be able to plan for that. I was confident that it is God who is behind me finding the "pink flat" so easily and so I started to pray that God would show me how to finance it. I prayed, and I prayed, and I asked others to pray, I had often heard and read accounts of how God had provided money in amazing ways for peoples' needs and I was expectant.

It was the Friday before I was due to pick up the keys at nine o'clock the next morning and I did not have anything like enough money. I even bought a lottery ticket!!! Nothing. I was scared and bewildered. I stood across the road from the agents' office at five to nine the next morning and could only think of one remaining option. God had not come through, so I had to help myself. With trembling knees and a very heavy heart, I went to the cash point right there and used a credit card to withdraw a large sum of money on credit. I felt ashamed, a failure and sick to my stomach when I thought of the need to repay it. I collected the keys and signed the contract.

I retrieved my furniture and household goods from people's garages where they had been stored for almost two years. It was great to see familiar objects again! It's not that they were particularly valuable or special, but they were familiar; they were mine and they held memories and even a sense of identity. It was not Ideal Home, but it was my own space, and I was grateful to have that back at last. The flat had a couple of redeeming features: it was reasonably spacious and had the most amazing view which afforded incredible sunsets to the West. There were many times in the years ahead when I would be reduced to tears of awe at the spectacular western skies. I was so often reminded that "He is coming on the clouds" Revelation 1:7.

The rent I was now contracted to pay was average for the area at that time, but it was well over half of my monthly salary so together with paying the council tax, energy and water etc plus the cost of my now considerable debt my monthly outgoings were crippling.

Having said that, there are comparatively few households in the UK at the moment that are entirely free from debt. It is a way of life for many, an accepted norm. However, I was by now a publicly committed Christian and I knew that being in debt in the way I was was not pleasing to God. The Bible has a lot to say about borrowing and lending and does not directly label that as sin at all, but it does speak wisdom into the situation *"The rich rule over the poor and the borrower is slave to the lender" Proverbs 22:7*

And I knew that Jesus had died a sacrificial death on a Roman cross to set me free. And I longed to embody that in every area of my life. As you will see from the next chapter, this was actually a time of tremendous fulfilment spiritually, and yet this financial situation never left my consciousness. Apart from the continual background anxiety about paying the bills and the sense of being "less than" when I couldn't afford most of life's extracurricular activities, I struggled with the sense that I could have done better; should have done better to manage finances and then I wouldn't be in this place. My two closest friends were widows as I have mentioned previously and had been more than adequately provided for by their late husbands; I also had a couple of other divorced women friends who had had very healthy divorce settlements that kept them provided for. Clearly those scenarios did not apply to me, and I felt a failure as a consequence. Somewhere along the line I felt I had failed.

And yet, two years previously, I had ascertained that I could have qualified for a mortgage, and I had in good faith asked God to show me the right flat to buy with the finance available, but despite viewing a number of flats, I had had no sense that God was in any of them. And yet, again, the very first potential rented property that I view and it's obvious that God is making a way. I don't understand.

As I look back over my multiple journal entries from that time, I am reminded clearly of how much this constant financial stress burdened me. I continually bounced between my growing assurance about God's purposes in my life and a deep sense of shame because I was not financially viable. A growing confidence that God's promises were always kept and that He had made some specific promises to me; and a sense of injustice because as a couple we had given up our home in the first place in response to a sense of obedience to His call, and because He had allowed my marriage to end leaving me with nothing but two (wonderful!) children, some furniture and a dog!! In other words, in this area of my life I was not at peace! It was like living with a threatening storm! In some ways, I looked back at the couple of years before the divorce when I had no income at all and thought it was actually easier than juggling a budget that was not enough!

One particular time of prayer comes to mind from this period. I was praying with three friends when I became aware that I was dancing with Jesus. As they say on "Strictly Come Dancing" we were dancing "in hold", something approaching a Viennese Waltz! Above our heads was a beautiful rainbow. At some point I reached up and grabbed the rainbow and then I was dancing on my own using the rainbow in the same way that gymnasts use ribbons in a floor exercise. And then a storm blew up and I could see trees around me bending almost double in the strength of the wind. I hung on to my rainbow for dear life and was tossed backwards and forwards by the currents but managed to hang on to it. At last, the storm blew out and I sank exhausted onto the ground and slowly the rainbow fluttered down and lay over me, covering and protecting me. This vision lasted some time, and my friends realised I was experiencing something in the Spirit and left me quietly to open my eyes again.

As I pondered that very real experience, I felt the dancing with Jesus represented partnership with him and the rainbow surely represents the promise of God as in Genesis after the flood. Despite the storms of life, I needed to hang on to those promises and never let go. And they would be my covering, my place of safety and rest.

However, seven years on, and I was still in the same position. My life seemed to be one of two halves. In the one half, God was teaching me and blessing me and encouraging me (see the next chapter) but in the other half, I was stressed and ashamed and exhausted. It came up to that time of year when I needed to renew my contract once again on the flat and I had been warned that the rent was going up. A couple of excerpts from my journals at the time paint the story:

"27th July 2004

I spent a fairly wretched weekend; not feeling to well- just tired and achy ,- and struggling with the inevitable disappointment that there has been no "return" of the misappropriated Euro 100 note. I think reality set in with a vengeance and I found myself confronting the continual financial battle – the increased rent from September, tiredness from being back at work and very much "in the deep end" at church with the Senior Pastors away on sabbatical for another 6 weeks. I so desperately want something to change. The summer is flying by and I long for freedom. A garden, BBQs and a dog" Another year seems set to pass without answers or any intervention from God.

My faith levels are low – not least of all because the amount of pastoral "giving out" since I got back from holiday; and I feel somewhat depressed. I spent some of the weekend bleating and pleading with God and begging Him to speak to me. Nothing.

Yesterday morning (Monday) I was late for the office (not feeling physically great) and I "snatched" a look at my Daily Light on the way out. I knew it was relevant but didn't have time to take it in. At a suitable time in the office, I, looked up Daily Light on the internet (never done that before!). The version I found was in the old King James text and read like this:

By faith Abraham, ... called to go out into a place which he should after receive for an inheritance, obeyed. Heb. 11:8
He shall choose our inheritance for us. Psa. 47:4
He led him about, he instructed him, he kept him as the apple of his eye. As an eagle stirreth up her nest, fluttereth over her young, spreadeth abroad her wings, taketh them, beareth them on her wings: so the LORD alone did lead him, and there was no strange god with him. Deut. 32:10-12
I am the LORD thy God which teacheth thee to profit, which leadeth thee by the way that thou shouldest go. Isa. 48:17
Who teacheth like Him? Job 36:22
We Walk by faith, not by sight. II Cor. 5:7
Here have we no continuing city, but we seek one to come. Heb. 13:14

Dearly beloved, I beseech you as strangers and pilgrims, abstain from fleshly lusts, which war against the soul. I Pet. 2:11

Arise ye and depart; for this is not your rest: because it is polluted, it shall destroy you, even with a sore destruction. Micah 2:10

The less familiar language challenged me. On the back of the desperation and self-pity I had been feeling at the weekend, these scriptures speak to me today as follows:

- *Like Abraham, God has called me to "go out" by faith (from providing myself with a home) and trust him for "my inheritance". This started in 1996 when I left the fellowship house.*
- *He has chosen and inheritance / a home for me*
- *The Lord has led me through eight years – in some ways of extreme difficulty; in some ways of extreme blessing*
- *He has taught me a great deal*
- *It is a renews challenge that I chose in 1996 – to walk by faith and not by sight.*
- *There has been "no strange god" with me. This is very important. It's the first tome this has struck me but I am suddenly confident that this is confirmation*

> *and answer to many prayers that I am not under any deceptive influences any more*
> - *That where I am in this flat at the moment is not "a continuing city"*
> - *And then finally the challenge: don*
> - *T stop where you are in this negative, self-pitying, anxious place! Its not aplace of rest! It's a place of destruction! Move on!*

Father God, I choose to repent of my wrong attitudes of self-pit, anxiety, frustration and doubt. I choose to lay them down at the foot of the cross and walk away in a different direction. Father, I choose to pick up again, by faith, the calling you have given me to trust you and to walk in it. Please forgive me for my rebellion and please cleanse me and renew me by the blood of Jesus shed for me. Please strengthen me to continue the race with my eyes fixed on Jesus. Thank you, Father, for speaking to me and I accept and am grateful for the rebuke. It shows you love me. Amen.

Wednesday August 11th 2004

Here I am Lord at a crossroads experience. And I'm sure the way forward is submission, but its hard. I can whinge and moan and subconsciously refuse to accept it. I can wait to "feel better" about it. Or I can choose to submit.

Choose to trust your sovereignty.

Choose to trust your perfect plan.

Choose to trust your timing

Choose to submit to these developments as part of your plan for me.

Lord, it's hard. But in the end its no choice. What can I do but choose to submit. "Humble myself under the mighty hand of God that he may exalt me in due course".

I know how easy it would be for you to release me from it all Lord. Part of me thinks perhaps you will. Part of me thinks I've thought that too many times already. Most of me knows that there's no reason why you should. All of me knows I need to make a decision now, Before I know what you might or might not have done, a decision based on the facts as they are now.

I choose to submit to your sovereignty in my life. I choose to accept with bowed head and quiet heart. I submit to your hand in my life.

But I do ask for your grace. I do ask that you will enable me to do what I cannot do in my own strength. I do ask that having made my own choice and my decision, my feelings will come in line with it.

The Lord gives and the Lord takes away. Thank you, Father, Amen".

God did not rescue me by providing large sums of cash in a miraculous fashion! I'm sure that happens sometimes! No, I lived with that anxiety for a long time learning to balance it with the favour being shown to me in so many ways in other areas. I was truly repentant for what I saw as my failings in this area – what I needed was to learn to receive the forgiveness that follows repentance. And whilst I was in no way punished for my perceived failures, I did not escape the consequences either. In due course I faced them by applying for and receiving an Independent Voluntary Agreement (IVA) which draws a line under any remaining debt, agrees settlements with each debtor which provides a manageable payment of one sum per month for five years. It was a tough schedule, but I duly completed the IVA and emerged debt free and thankfully remain that way.

Thankfully God's word is full of characters who were not perfect! And yet, they were significant in God's purposes and were included in His plans. Many of us identify with the disciple Peter in the gospels as the one who often got it wrong, particularly when he denied knowing Jesus on the night of the trial, and yet Jesus apparently knew that Peter's heart was repentant and was at pains to re-establish Peter's calling with him in John Chapter 21. David in the Old Testament was a hero when he defeated Goliath but messed up badly over a woman called Bathsheba (2 Samuel 23). He nevertheless came to a place of repentance and goes down in history overall as "a man after God's own heart".

Such is grace. The undeserved favour and love of God Almighty, maker of Heaven and Earth and Father of our Lord Jesus Christ.

Afterthought: "You can't be in debt and win. It doesn't work". Dave Ramsey

Chapter 16: Singing a new song

"Sing to the Lord a new song…" Psalm 96:1

That picture of the bird in the cage given so many years ago by the Bishop from Nigeria was becoming very real to me. After the night in my living room, when the Lord spoke so clearly to me and I left the church I had been part of for over ten years and went to SWLV, I identified clearly with the bird who on flying from the cage flew into a field of grain and fed and fed and fed on the food. For two years I fed; on good teaching, wonderful worship, servant evangelism, prayer, prophecy and some really good training opportunities.

After two years, when I was really feeling that I had got to grips with so many changes and challenges, it was announced that a new church was being planted out from SWLV into the town in which I lived!! Oh no! My heart sank! I scarcely had to pray about it; I guessed that was going to mean me moving on too!

In due course the first meeting of the new church was convened in the home of the young couple who were going to be the Senior Pastors, and I went along. There were twelve of us there. They were expecting their third child, and my second grandchild had just been born! However, they had a clear sense of God's calling to plant the church in our town and a passion to see the Kingdom of God extended. We met as a group midweek in their home for several months and other people gradually started to join us as word got around. Meanwhile on Sundays, I continued to go back to SWLV. Vineyard churches are entirely self-funded so it was a few months before we could finance hiring a location for Sunday meetings. Our first two Sunday gatherings were held in the local Holiday Inn, but there was a new secondary school being built in the town and our Senior Pastor was able to contact the headmaster designate and agree our use of the school hall and classrooms on Sunday mornings. So, when the brand-new school opened its gates for the first time to pupils for the September term, our embryo church moved in for Sunday mornings and it has been our Sunday home ever since.

J&B the Senior Pastors of the new church were intentional in getting to know the individual members of their embryo congregation and I had several meetings with them in the first couple of months of the new church. I was completely honest with them about my life and all its circumstances, and they were so loving and affirming. Gradually word spread about our church plant and people started turning up. The very first Sunday meeting that we had at the Holiday Inn our Senior Pastor did everything! He put the chairs out, led worship and preached! I served coffee! There were probably about two dozen of us. But by the time the new school was completed and opened, we seemed to meet more and more people week by week. Our Senior Pastor was bi-vocational for at least a couple of years until we had grown enough in numbers to be able to finance a salary. His secular role was a taxing and stressful one and in that first couple of years the demands of a 40+ hours a week professional job in London, plus leading, pastoring and teaching in the new church, plus the usual demands of three very young children and family life were overwhelming for both him and his wife. His physical health suffered and not long in, he suffered a full mental breakdown. The underlying damage from his own very dysfunctional and traumatic childhood began to surface and the stress of bi-vocational living and the responsibilities of a church congregation were a weight which pressed down until cracks began to appear and our Pastor went into breakdown. This could well have been the end of our church plant. But it wasn't. In many ways it was the true beginning.

The church was still small enough to be quite intimate. Everybody knew everybody and because our Senior Pastor had aways emphasised the values of open realism, acceptance and non-judgement, that was how our little church responded to this crisis. Our Pastor himself never missed a Sunday. He stood in front of the church regularly and truthfully week by week and we honoured and respected him and his wife for it.

We prayed, and supported, and prayed some more. What we had no idea about at the time was that we were involved with a real live Kintsugi process going on in our Pastor's life. Kintsugi, if you are not familiar with the term, roughly translates as "joining with gold" and is the ancient Japanese repair technique which uses urushi lacquer dusted with powdered gold to restore broken ceramic and porcelain vessels. I can only say that with hindsight. At the time, it was deeply concerning, causing us as a fellowship to pray, and to step up, and to contribute to the laying of our foundation as a Christ-centred community. Now I realise that in order for this young man to achieve the desire of his heart and pastor a church that would lead others into the fullness of their salvation, he himself had to be broken and then re-made by God's grace and the healing power of the cross of Christ. The (almost) finished vessel does not hide its broken past but boasts in the enhanced beauty of its healing as what were the lines of brokenness are mended with gold which catches the light and reflects it.

That broken young man, almost thirty years on, is one of the wisest, deepest, gentlest men you could wish to know. Whilst building and pastoring our church he eventually studied for and obtained two separate doctorates; a Doctorate in Ministry and a PhD in Theology and having pastored for twenty-seven years now lectures and consults in various areas of church and culture. And I would say that he has been the most profoundly affirming and encouraging influence in my own life to date. A male influence in my life that has actually not betrayed or let me down!

Our new church continued to grow, and I was privileged to become increasingly involved in it. Witnessing our Pastor receive help and deal with his foundational brokenness emphasised for me many of the things I had begun learning about at SWLV. The fact that we are all broken people to some extent or another and we are broken because we all live in a broken world that has fallen far short of the blueprint that a Creator God had when the world was new. None of us have grown up around perfect people, be they parents, siblings, teachers, or peers. We have none of us fully known the security of affirmation or the confidence of assured identity. In the 21st century we are bombarded by the pain of suffering and the stress of continual wars and the tensions of racial and religious differences. Many of us paste over our cracks to the best of our ability, but I had experienced by now the enduring, sustaining, healing love of God which was bringing me continually through the years of rejection and betrayal and self-doubt to a better place. A place in which I had refused the identity of victim and chosen to allow Truth and Love beyond myself to begin to restore me. And I wanted to share that. To encourage others that God did not just heal bodies (although He does!) but he heals souls and spirits as well. I wanted to serve. And that was what our Pastor and his lovely wife saw in me and encouraged.

With their encouragement, I began to train and build a small team of people to pray for others in twos or threes in prophetic, intercessory prayer seeking God for healing for the roots to longstanding anxieties and fears that surface in our adult lives and people in the fellowship began to respond and book appointments. It was a big part of a "be real" culture. We discouraged each other from hiding behind platitudes and excuses on the basis that we remember that nothing is hidden from God so best to get on and deal with it! An oft quoted Vineyard saying is "Come just as you are but don't stay as you are!". The assumption is that if you meet Jesus, you will start to change!!

As we continued to grow as a congregation, we developed a voluntary leadership team out of the congregation to support the Pastors, and I am humbled to say that, despite the fact that many of my own cracks were still very obvious, I had the privilege of being part of that for twenty- five years or so. It was hard work, challenging, rewarding and at times very stressful!

The church continued to grow and thrive, and I was increasingly aware that I was "singing a new song"; one I could never have taught myself; one that was more subtle and nuanced than the first song I sang. And I was no longer stuck in the field feeding avidly, but there was now a freedom to fly and let my song be heard.

And so the years continued to roll on by and I was blessed to be part of so many adventures. One of the earlier ones was to go with our whole leadership team at the time on a day's workshop to discover what makes us tick personality wise. I was dreading it! I anticipated being revealed for who I really was, and all my insecurities kicked in. The model we were using on this occasion was the Myers Briggs Type Indicator (there are others, and we tried a variety over the years!). My fears turned to fascination as I began to understand that this is not about judgement but about appreciation of the differences in our sources of energy, the kind of information we prefer, how we make decisions and how we relate to the external world. And the key word for me was "differences". We so often misunderstand this word! We attach inferences to the word that are pejorative. We turn it into a word of judgement. But "different" does not mean "better" and it does not mean "worse"! It means "diverse", "disparate" "different". And I realised that "different" is OK! I'm not supposed to be a clone of anybody else! I am different! I am me! The "me" created in the image of God and I need to embrace who I am and not model myself on anybody else. This was a huge step in my journey of self-understanding, self-acceptance and self-confidence. It was also hugely helpful in understanding other people and helping me be far more tolerant of how and why they are "different" to me! Not better, not worse, just different!

I was gaining confidence in my new song but not quite enough to be singing from the tallest tree in the forest yet! And then I began to discover that there were always nefrains to learn to that new song.

Afterthought: "The purpose of learning is growth, and our minds, unlike our bodies, can continue growing as long as we live" Mortimer Adler

Chapter 17: Melodies, Harmonies and Rhythms

"Blessed be the God and Father of our Lord Jesus Christ"
Ephesians 3:1

There's a big responsibility on the small congregation of a newly planted church to pray! And the Lord moved in mysterious ways to lay the foundation of prayer in our little church.

At the very first preliminary gathering of the proposed church, my friend Margie and I met a third lady called Eileen who had been recently widowed and had moved from her locality of many years into our area and had heard about the new church plant and the three of us became very close friends for many years. And from the beginning we began to pray together. We were all single, Margie was also widowed, and although I was the only one still working, we managed to get together very regularly to pray including before the service on Sundays. We were sometimes joined by others on that occasion, but we were so often seen around together that we became known as

"The three Musketeers"! We were down at a conference in Bournemouth once and even the girl on the reception desk of the hotel once referred to us as "the three musketeers!" And so we were for a while until we were joined by the most unlikely fourth member. Bill had turned up at the church one Sunday and started showing up regularly, but our paths didn't really cross until we had a first church weekend away in Kent. There was a time of prayer over the weekend and somehow the three of us ended up at the end of the meeting, chatting to Bill and we got into talking about prayer. Bill was a single guy, a bit younger than us and working as a mental health nurse. He made it very clear that he was a recovering alcoholic with a bit of a chequered background but that he had known Jesus for a while and had a heart to pray.

That was the beginning of a somewhat extraordinary period of a year or so in all our lives. We found that we had a powerful synergy in praying together and it became the focus of our corporate free time. Bill did not have life sorted by any means and yet he had an acute awareness of spiritual atmosphere and would often experience visions in the Spirit. Together we were led into some deep times of intercessory prayer for God's purposes for the church and for our town. It was such a blessing to be in God's presence in a strong sense of unity and power. I learned a lot about praying following the leading of the Spirit rather than praying my own thoughts and ideas. We called ourselves "Gatekeepers" because we realised that one of us lived on the north of our town, one on the south, one on the east and one on the west! We were aware of Isaiah 62:6 *"I have set watchmen on your walls, O Jerusalem, which shall never hold their peace nor day nor night"* and we had a strong sense of calling and responsibility. We spent hours and hours in prayer together. And then it stopped. Bill was beginning to struggle with alcohol again and we encouraged him to go into rehab after which he did not come back to our town. We stayed in touch for a while, but it seemed that season was over.

I continue to explore the realms of this thing called prayer! I have learned a lot about the many, many facets that there are to it and remain convinced that I continue to scratch the surface. It is a lifelong apprenticeship. And the most enormous privilege.

In 2010 I went on mission! Our church had been building links with churches in Colombo, Sri Lanka since the 2004 Tsunami, and we had already sent three teams out on short term missions where we had provided practical as well as spiritual support. I was excited but apprehensive about going. The leader of the team was very comprehensive in our preparation. There were 10 of us going, three women and seven guys of varying ages and the nature of the accommodation was uncertain. We certainly weren't staying in hotels. We were being prepared for dealing with unfamiliar living conditions, practical hard work, being practised in sharing our testimonies…. and anything else that cropped up! We were running a small conference for pastors, and I was down to do some teaching. There was plenty to be apprehensive about!

Before we left there were various opportunities to be prayed for as a team and as individuals. It has stuck in my memory that during those final preparation weeks, on three disparate occasions three quite different people gave me the scripture from Psalm 81 *"Open wide your mouth and I will fill it"*. I don't know what that brings to mind for you. It might have been about food – but as I pondered it, I felt it was a reassurance about having the right words at the right time, and I pondered what that might mean. Colombo was hot and humid, busy and bustling. Our accommodation whilst we were in the city was a small 3 bedroomed flat – for 10 of us! The people were lovely and so humbling as they had so little and were so joyful in God. We attended their church services; we visited homegroups in the evenings in threes and fours held in tiny, tiny houses in alleys that no vehicles could access and filled with so many people that they spilled into the alleys. We gave our testimonies there and watched in amazement as people queued to be prayed for by us at the end. One morning we ladies were told to be up early because we had been invited to an early morning ladies' prayer meeting at the church. No problem. Until we got there, and I found that I was leading it although none of the ladies that would be present spoke English; and my Tamil…. Well!! Then I remembered "Open your mouth and I will fill it"! And I prayed "Lord if I open my mouth…. well, please, please will you fill it"! And He did and I have made that my prayer so many times since!

In 2012 I at last retired from Crown Agents. I had enjoyed my job but there were so many other things that I wanted to do. Once I retired, I was asked to officially join the staff team of the church on what the Anglicans would call a non-stipendiary basis, and I accepted. I spent a very busy but satisfying ten years in that role through many ups and downs, with many wonderful opportunities and working alongside some wonderful people. Its hard work running a thriving church.

In 2017 the national Association of Vineyard Churches UK & Ireland announced that they planned to train some Spiritual Directors for their Senior Pastors. It was to be a year's training course to qualify, and applications were invited. The training was to be very heavily subsidised by the Association on the understanding that once trained you would be available to serve Senior Pastors for two years. I felt very privileged to be selected as part of the first cohort of 12 to train. Spiritual Directors help people find their own way to deepen and strengthen their relationship with the Godhead. They walk alongside believers without judgement or direction, helping them to discern their own way forward. I thoroughly enjoyed the training. Our cohort were a wonderful bunch of people from across the country and we quickly formed close and deep relationships. There was a lot of reading, which I enjoyed, some writing, and in our occasional residential sessions together, we were led in practising compassionate, discerning listening to God, ourselves and each other through contemplative exercises, and experience of receiving and giving spiritual direction individually and in groups. I loved it.

However, 10 months or so into the year, there was a change of plan. The course was being extended from one year to two in order for students to achieve a suitable qualification. We were invited to think about whether or not we wanted to continue, although the practical arrangements around the second year of training would be very different to the first. I was hesitant. And disappointed. I had committed a year. Over some weeks I pondered my decision and of course prayed, seeking God's purpose rather than my own and still I felt really uneasy about re-committing to another year. I wasn't sure why, but the feeling of unease wouldn't shift. And yet I don't consider myself to be a quitter. If I commit to something, I see it though. I talked it over with my Pastor from the point of view of our church's investment, and he assured me that it was my decision completely. I eventually went off to our next residential weekend, when decisions would be required, feeling very much at odds with myself. That was not helped when it became clear that the other eleven members of the cohort were choosing to continue. I really felt in a turmoil.

During our morning session, we had been together as a group with our trainer discussing a topic and were to go away for an hour on our own to process our thoughts. As we broke up, I popped up to my room for something and to use the bathroom. All morning, I had had an odd phrase running through my brain, which seemed really out of place. I was learning that when that happens it is often Holy Spirit bringing something to my attention. The phrase was "grafted in" and my only association was a childhood memory of being in the garden with my father whilst he was talking to a neighbour over the fence about how this neighbour was "grafting in" a cutting from one species of apple tree onto another. Literally as I sat on the loo, a picture formed in my mind of the same thing happening to grape vines; and as it did, I clearly felt the voice of Holy Spirit speaking into my thoughts

"You see, Wendy, you are not a pure blend wine! "

What???? And again

"You are a mixed blend wine; a Cabernet Sauvignon Shiraz (my favourite!!!); And I want you to move on."

Well! My turmoil settled and I knew what I had to do.

As I pondered that decision, I realised that much as I had enjoyed learning new ways of walking alongside fellow believers, I would not be happy about using that particular, fairly formal discipline exclusively. I still loved to sit with people informally and wait on the Lord with them to pray healing or revelation or understanding with them as Holy Spirit leads. Similarly, I had just recruited and trained a team of people in our church in the ministry of Sozo, * which I also love to witness working with people to bring them into new dimensions of freedom and relationship with the member of the Trinity. I gradually became very comfortable with the understanding that the Lord equips us with many different tools in our tool bags for the journey of transformation. Some of us are best suited in our personalities to become specialists with one particular tool, whilst others are better suited to handling a variety! If I'm really honest though, deep down I still struggled that I had opted out of that commitment and somehow wasted what had been offered me as a privileged opportunity.

Interestingly, just a couple of months later, a friend introduced me to a wonderful series of books by the American author Sharon Garlough Brown, * written as novels about a random group of Christian women who happen to all sign up to the same spiritual retreat. The novels journey with them as they learn together about spiritual formation; how that impacts their life journeys and understanding of what it is to walk with Jesus and how their different life circumstances are then impacted. In turn I shared the books with a couple of close friends in church and I suddenly found myself organising groups of four and five women who were meeting together regularly to read the books and share their own journeys together as they learned. All of a sudden, I was facilitating spiritual formation across (mostly) the women in our church and God was blessing us with an insight into spiritual direction and all those particular tools! So, maybe my cut-short Spiritual Direction training was not wasted! God moves in mysterious ways…..

And so my new song continues with varied melodies, harmonies and rhythms and my confidence to sing it from higher trees has grown. Our heavenly Father has such wealth of treasures to share with us. We are blessed indeed.

Afterthought: "Anyone who stops learning is old, whether at twenty or eighty. Anyone who keeps learning stays young!" Henry Ford

*Sensible Shoes" by Sharon Garlough Brown published by IVP books

**Sozo Bethel Sozo is a unique inner healing and deliverance ministry that helps deepen your relationship with God. See www.bethelsozo.org.uk

Chapter 18: A home that no-one can take away.

"My thought are not your thoughts nor my ways your ways" declares the Lord" Isaiah 55:8

Its 2019 and I have been in the "pink" flat for twenty-one years. I had been grateful for a roof over my head and for the fact that the rent had not increased as much during that time as it could have done. However, I had never felt "permanent" there. There had been no money spent on it during that time, and that was beginning to show. In fact, twice during my time there I had been advised that the owners wanted to sell; twice I had shown estate agents over; and on one occasion prospective purchasers too. Both occasions came to nothing, but as you can imagine it was pretty disturbing!

And then in August 2019, with absolutely no warning, I received through the post a Section 21 notice to evict, sometimes referred to as a "no fault eviction". Here we go again: enforced house move number five! First Holly Hill, then the fellowship house, our home for almost twenty years, then my brother's, then the old lady's house and now the pink flat! And way back, when I was leaving the fellowship house, what was it that I did eventually tell God when He asked what I really wanted? "Lord, I just want a home that nobody can take away from me".

I stood with the envelope in my hand feeling cold with dread. I was now in my seventies and just the prospect of moving was daunting, but the immediate understanding of the implications was deeply alarming. I was abreast of the current accommodation prices in my area, i.e. horrendously high! And I had six weeks to vacate! To cap it all, in the middle of that six weeks I was going on a fully booked two-week river cruise that was a gift from a family member.

I sat with this letter in my hand, and I could feel the panic rising. Over the next couple of days, I battled with huge doubts and fears. My fears were very real about where I would end up living. I knew the local area well and knew it would take a miracle. And speaking of miracles, I was struggling with some doubts about where the Lord's purpose was in all this. Over all these years, His constant word and encouragement to me was to trust Him. And on the one hand, He had never honestly let me down, and yet I was struggling with the fact that back in 1996 when I was told I had to leave the fellowship house, and I was still earning, and I could have got a mortgage to buy, it would have been so easy for him to facilitate that by leading me to see an appropriate flat to buy! He had done exactly that two years later when I was driven to look for one to rent! And I had consequently spent 20 years paying thousands of pounds in rent which would have paid off a mortgage! How does that make any sense? "Lord, help me understand! Where are you in this? You have taught me to trust you; I have sought to trust you; but it seems to go from bad to worse." So went the pattern of my mental struggle for those first couple of days. The sense of failure was looming over me again. Here I was in the last season of my life, and I couldn't provide a home for myself. That feels like failure.

I did some practical stuff. I went to the Citizens' Advice Bureau; I researched property websites; I talked with family and friends and I asked close friends to pray. And then I went off on the holiday that I had been so looking forward to and practised leaving my worries and anxieties at the foot of the cross daily, hourly sometimes, and prayed for the blood of Jesus to sanctify them. I had a brilliant holiday!!

Way back in the early '90s when I was at SWL Vineyard church, I had met Martha, and we became very good friends. She was a single woman, a bit younger than me, and at that time we were both working full time. We found we prayed together very well and met quite regularly together after work to share a meal and spend some time in prayer. We continued in that after I left SWLV until she got married, when her circumstances obviously changed and, whilst we always kept in regular touch, we did not spend as much time together. When I returned from holiday, I was keen to contact her because I knew her brother, to whom she was very close, was desperately ill. We had a telephone conversation in which she updated me and asked me to pray, and I also updated her on my eviction situation. I now had three weeks left of my notice to quit. We stayed in touch by text and over the next few days her brother sadly lost his battle for life.

Meanwhile, by previous arrangement, I had gone up to see my daughter and her family in Nottingham for the weekend. I still had no idea what I was going to do but was beginning to think that my furniture would have to go into storage and I would have to stay with friends / family until the way forward was clear. I felt heavy and insecure but somehow, I was managing to choose to keep trusting God.

It was August Bank Holiday weekend and on the Sunday afternoon I was with my family in a large local park on their annual church picnic! The scene is so clear in my memory. The weather was warm and dry, there was noise and laughter all around as dozens of families came together to have fun, I was sitting on a rug on the grass, and my phone rang. I checked who it was, and it was Martha, so I answered, aware that she was deeply grieving. And there, sitting on the grass surrounded by left over sandwiches and drinks, kids' toys and excited dogs, my life changed.

Martha was ringing to tell me that the Lord wanted her to offer me a maisonette that an aunt to left her a few years before as a home. She explained that she had wanted to offer it to me for a long time – long before my current crisis - and that she couldn't. But that something had happened on the day her brother died which meant that she now could. She has never told me what exactly happened. And furthermore, the Lord had shown her that she was to offer it to me at the same rent that I had been paying, for the rest of my life, and with a guarantee of no rent increase, ever. I was dumbfounded; absolutely dumbfounded.

Because of all the noise around me and because I needed to talk to my daughter and son-in-law, I thanked her profusely and suggested I get back to her.

My mind was buzzing. There was immediately absolutely no doubt for me that this was God! None whatsoever! However, I'm ashamed to admit that my rejoicing was not immediate. I was cautious. I wasn't sure it was what I wanted…… but then I was in no position to choose, was I? But part of me wanted to choose. I hadn't had the freedom to do that since we chose to sell up and move to Holly Hill. My head was acknowledging that this had to be the way forward. My heart was some way behind.

I spoke to Martha again later. I knew roughly where the maisonette was – very close to my existing location in fact. I remembered when she had been left it and had debated about whether to sell straight away or retain it to rent out. I remembered that she had decided to keep it, spent a lot of money updating it and I knew she had it let to tenants. I accepted her amazing offer and we discussed the legalities of how she proposed protecting my right to stay there at an unchanging rent. Unfortunately, because she had to give the existing tenants a month's notice to quit, the dates would not work out for me to move straight in. OK. Something to pray about! She also suggested that I liaise with the managing agents locally and arrange to go in for a viewing.

My heart was still having a struggle to catch up with my head, but with two weeks to eviction date, I didn't really have time to worry about that! There was a lot to do! However, I still had six weeks to provide for in between the two addresses. That was the priority area for prayer. I had some kind offers from friends and family to go and stay….. and then amazingly, a close friend's son who was in the process of preparing a flat to go on the market, having just moved out of it, suggested that I could move in there for the six weeks. It was still furnished and very close to my existing location so…. it was another answer to prayer!!

Meanwhile, I arranged to go and visit the maisonette with the managing agent and a friend. I had no idea what to expect. It was difficult. The existing tenants were there; the managing agent was in a hurry, and I was uncomfortable. I felt bad that a family was being evicted in order that I could move in; I couldn't really take in the details – my friend did better – but I felt it was smaller than my existing flat and that I would have to get rid of furniture. Overall, I was still very grateful, but not overwhelmingly happy!

Moving is such hard work! By the time all my furniture had been packed and taken into storage, I'd cleaned the place thoroughly; faced a battle with that agent to get my original deposit back and moved into my temporary dwelling, I was exhausted. And six weeks later, it was happening all over again. With the help of my wonderful daughter and some equally wonderful friends, I moved into my forever home.

The day before I was scheduled to move in, we had been able to pick up the keys and for the first time I had the opportunity to properly inspect the maisonette. It was on the ground floor, with a garden both front and back and set in a very pleasant residential road. When we opened the front door, we were greeted with a strong and not very pleasant smell! We quickly worked out that it was the smell of wet carpet, and all the carpets had been cleaned and were still drying. Furthermore, I was expecting there to be wall damage as one of the few things I had noted on my flying visit was that there was a wall mounted TV in the living room and various things on other walls. However, the walls were now immaculate throughout and clearly had been both filled and re-painted. So far so good! (I had been very relieved to hear that the existing tenants had found another property close by and were happy – an answer to prayer!)

The next day the furniture was delivered, and I was moving in! I had to admit that I was surprised that everything actually fitted in rather well and with a little help from my friends and family it all started to take shape. I remember going to church the first Sunday and finding myself saying to someone who'd asked how the new home was that it "fitted like a glove". And it did!

As I write, that is exactly five years ago to the day, and I have been so blessed to be here! Within four months of moving in we were all in Covid lockdown. For the first time in more than twenty years I had a garden; spring 2020 was a beautiful one and I spent so many of the solitary hours on the patio in the sunshine watching the garden come back to life. I have apple trees and conifers, a shed and a greenhouse and a myriad of birds. I am surrounded by trees, and it is sometimes so quiet that the birdsong sounds like a symphony orchestra. I daily thank God for Martha and whatever happened to change her circumstances at exactly the right time for me. I still sometimes struggle that I'm not a homeowner with an estate to leave my children, then I remember that Jesus wasn't a homeowner either and I am content. My heart caught up at last.

Afterthought: "You will make mistakes, disappoint God and others, and have days when you wonder why God ever called you in the first place. Don't despair! Your usefulness to God is based on His consistency not yours!" Jeff Iorg

Chapter 19: And this is now

"He who began a new work in you will carry it on to completion…Philippians 1:6

I'm a little surprised and very grateful that we have actually reached the last chapter together! It's been a bit of a journey, hasn't it, and it's great to have shared it with you.

As I write, I am still living in my forever home with great joy and thankfulness; I am still part of the same wonderful church family, although I have handed over some of my responsibilities. I'm learning the lessons of facing old age and not enjoying all of them; and I have a great sense of wanting to maximise whatever time I have left to prepare for heaven; I want to "die climbing" as my former pastor used to say.

My wonderful children have raised three wonderful grandchildren, who have been a great joy from the time they were newborn babies through to the confident and successful adults that they are now. I was determined to be an involved grandparent and I think have managed to do that despite the fact that two of them have always lived a couple of hundred miles away and I only saw them every few weeks, although it was quality time because it would be for a few days at a stretch and I was then able to be part of their daily routine, whereas the other grandchild has always lived locally, and I have seen her much more regularly, but for short periods of time, supporting her parents wherever I could as they both always worked full time whilst she was growing. I think my relationship with all three of them is as strong, despite the different basis of our relationships.

Because one of them is an only child, I felt strongly from an early age that I wanted as a grandparent to invest in their relationships with each other, so that they would love and trust and be there for each other each other all the way through their lives. To that end, I did all I could to get them together whenever possible, and we had many memorable summer holidays with the two families together hiking in the Borrowdale Valley with the walks getting longer as the kids legs got longer!

Being a mother taught me so much in the earlier years of my life and being a grandparent has also taught me much, including an understanding that my role is to support their parents, and that I'm not in control anymore; that my way is actually not the only way; and that the bonus of grandparenting is indeed being able to hand them back when you've had enough!

Now, with them all in their middle twenties, this book is very much for them. The Lord told me thirty years ago through someone who hardly knew me that I would write a book. I received that as a word from the Lord, although I had no idea what I would write about, and the timing hasn't been right until now. But as it all started coming together this year, I knew that to some extent, I was writing with them in mind. I wonder very seriously what sort of world and society they are going to be bringing their children into, and truly believe that along with everyone else, they will need a deep walk with God to cope. God is working His purposes out and the time is drawing near!

When I was the age that they are now, I was a wife and a mother of young children, and my biggest worry was balancing all the day-to-day responsibilities and tasks involved in running my home. My precious grandchildren at the same age live in a world that is more than ever torn by war; where forty years after Band Aid, we still are not feeding the world; where they are reminded daily that the planet's resources are running out; that Artificial Intelligence will take their jobs; and that there are not enough homes for them to own one. They live in a society that doesn't believe in an absolute truth anymore; that mostly has little idea why our yearly calendar is punctuated by events called Christmas and Easter; that struggles increasingly with mental health from an increasingly younger age; where misogyny is still rife; and where levels of violence and death amongst young people are appallingly high. I could go on. I didn't face all that at their age.

So, my hope and my prayer for my grandchildren is that they will each discover a commitment to journey with Jesus to a deep place of relationship with God and the reality of His alternative Kingdom; that the journey will be unique to each of them and at the right pace for their needs – but that it will be a bit faster in progress than mine! I had the privilege of meeting The Truth in my early twenties, and through my thirties, forties, fifties, sixties and seventies there has been much progress. But it feels to me like I learned the hard way. And to a large extent we all press into God when we are challenged or in pain, and life often provides that in measure! As Jesus tells his closest friends in John's gospel account *"In this world you will have tribulation…."* but He also tells them all the way through chapters 14,15 16 & 17 of John's account of the gospel (or "good news"), that He has overcome the world and then He shares wisdom and truth at length with them as to how they are empowered to live in that same overcoming power.

At the end of these chapters, which are actually an account of the last meal Jesus ever shared with his best friends; one of whom would go on to betray him, and the rest of whom would be responsible for taking his teaching to the whole of the then known world and, in doing so, found the 2000 year old Christian Church, Jesus prays for them at length. Amazingly, He also prays for us! For you, and for me! (John 17:20).

The British media are intent on telling us that the church in Britain is dying out. Is it? A church of two hundred is not really considered large now. Several of our cities have churches of several hundreds and just a few with vibrant congregations of well over a thousand. The average age of our population overall is aging fast, as we know. The average age in our churches is not. Thousands of young people across these islands were at Christian camping festivals this summer and will be next.

We live in challenging times, but exciting times. There is more research supporting the evidence for the historical existence of Jesus than ever, together with archaeological evidence and increased cultural understanding covering places and facts. We have more research into the original language of scripture and the history of its translation than ever before, and that printed word is available in more languages, editions, and formats than ever before. It remains the most widely sold book of all time. There is free access to teaching and church services online, as well as abundance of worship songs. And all those things are invaluable and constructive,

But my prayer for my children, my grandchildren, my friends and relations, my brothers and sisters in church, and for you my reader, is that our head knowledge will increase, and our understanding deepen, yes for sure. But above all my prayer is that they will grow in relationship with Father God, Jesus our Saviour and Holy Spirit our Advocate / Helper. That they will build that relationship as we do all relationships; by choosing to invest; by open communication, by trust, by being honest and by being persistent and growing faith.

In recent years, together with two very dear friends, I have been leading residential creative prayer retreats. The story of how God brought that about out of absolutely nowhere is amazing and maybe for another day. We call the retreat "Potbound". It came about originally immediately after the Covid pandemic when all of us had been so restricted, and it speaks to our need to make sure we don't stop growing because our roots. i.e. prayer relationship with God, have become stunted and need release. I do some teaching on creative ways to pray, and my two creative friends lead delegates wonderfully in ways to express emotion and even memories through crafting and painting with beautiful results.

I am overwhelmingly grateful that God in His fatherly love saw me as a young plant, a tender shoot, stifled by the pot in which I was planted and reaching, reaching for life and its meaning, but bruised over and over by the pot of my family, my education, the culture around me, the relationships I had ; limited by lack of understanding, lack of vision, lack of Truth, and because I didn't understand that, I had reached the limits of my boundaries!

Thanks be to God that He stepped in and turned my pot upside down! Literally tipped me out of my prison of unbelief and released me, re-potted me into a whole new world of understanding. He introduced me to a whole different soil! The soil of salvation! And a new container called Truth, in the shape of a Saviour! He took me in hand and began to ease out my cramped roots, releasing them to grow and produce upwards growth which flourished as it reached for life and light.

And my Father, the gardener, has re-potted me regularly in His efforts to keep me growing, healthy and fruitful. Yes, it's been uncomfortable at times, but looking back over fifty years of being tended, pruned, fed, transplanted, and indeed harvested, I would not have lived my life any other way. I am nearer the end than the beginning and have everything to look forward to. Yes, my body is feeling its age a bit! But my soul and my spirit are renewed daily and do not grow old.

I didn't always understand, I got some things wrong, but there has been forgiveness and restitution. There always is. One of the most recent bittersweet joys, is that my precious ex-husband came to the end of his life, which is sad. But the joy is that in his last few weeks, through our daughter, he found his faith again and recommitted himself to God. He will be in heaven, something I had prayed about for thirty years. Do you remember?

[15] Perhaps the reason he was separated from you for a little while was that you might have him back forever—[16] no longer………, but as a dear brother" Philemon

Choose to trust God and He will prove Himself faithful. Amen.

Afterthought: "You fill to the full with most beautiful splendour those souls who close their eyes that they may see" from The Cloud of Unknowing. Anon.

Printed in Great Britain
by Amazon